D1370164

SCOTT COUNTY LIBRARY
SAVAGE MN 55378

Hands-On
Ecology

Hands-On Ecology

Real-Life Activities for Kids

By

Colleen Kessler

Illustrated by Mike Eustis

Prufrock Press Inc.
Waco, Texas

Library of Congress Cataloging-in-Publication Data

Kessler, Colleen.
  Hands-on ecology : real-life activities for kids / by Colleen Kessler.
     p. cm.
  ISBN-13: 978-1-59363-201-4 (pbk.)
  ISBN-10: 1-59363-201-0 (pbk.)
  1. Ecology—Study and teaching (Elementary)—Activity programs. I. Title.

  QH541.2.K47 2006
  372.35'7—dc22

                            2006025835

Copyright ©2007 Prufrock Press Inc.

Edited by Lacy Elwood
Illustrated by Mike Eustis
Production Design by Marjorie Parker

ISBN-13: 978-1-59363-201-4
ISBN-10: 1-59363-201-0

The purchase of this book entitles the buyer to reproduce student activity pages for classroom use only. Other use requires written permission of publisher. All rights reserved.

At the time of this book's publication, all facts and figures cited are the most current available; all telephone numbers, addresses, and Web site URLs are accurate and active; all publications, organizations, Web sites, and other resources exist as described in this book; and all have been verified. The authors and Prufrock Press make no warranty or guarantee concerning the information and materials given out by organizations or content found at Web sites, and we are not responsible for any changes that occur after this book's publication. If you find an error or believe that a resource listed here is not as described, please contact Prufrock Press.

Prufrock Press Inc.
P.O. Box 8813
Waco, TX 76714-8813
Phone: (800) 998-2208
Fax: (800) 240-0333
www.prufrock.com

Table of Contents

Introduction

What Is Ecology?

No living thing exists in seclusion; all things need energy and materials from each other and the environments in which they live. The lives of all plants and animals affect the lives of the other organisms around them. *Ecology* is the study of the relationships between living things and the environments in which they live.

Ecologists need to have a strong background in a variety of scientific disciplines; therefore, studying this topic will provide kids with an overview of many threads. Disciplines like botany, zoology, and biology are important, as is a love of writing, speaking, and researching. Ecologists are charged with the responsibility of helping people to recognize and understand the connections all around them. We have an impact on the sustainability of those connections. Ecologists can work as consultants, research assistants, research scientists, and professors. Scientists studying the environment are also responsible for educating and influencing policymakers.

Ecologists conduct fieldwork to study populations in their natural environments and conduct specific laboratory experiments to analyze the chemical makeup of soil, water, air, and other conditions within the ecosystem. This helps them notice patterns and predict effects of human impact on the environment. They can use this information to plan ways of making changes and improvements.

Why Is Ecology an Important Field?

As concern for the well-being of the environment and the impact humans have on it rises, the demand for ecologists increases. As species become extinct, the global temperature rises, and tropical forests deplete, it becomes imperative that we raise a population ready to accept the challenge of turning environmental issues around and solving the problems that humans have created.

Concern over the environment is not new. Since ancient times, civilizations have faced ecological crises and have been forced to attempt solutions. In Ancient Greece, Italy, and Babylon, timbering (what we now call deforestation—the stripping of trees) caused citizens to use an early form of solar energy: They built their houses and other buildings so that they faced the sun and were able to absorb the warmth. In the 1600s, much of Europe was forced to switch to coal as their source of heat, because timbering was also depleting their forests. This switch to coal led to more air pollution.

In 1798, Thomas Malthus cautioned that if populations continued to rise, food and other natural resources would run out. His views were not popular, and he was thought of as a doomsayer. However, Charles Darwin and others recognized Malthus' writings as important contributions.

Living conditions continued to get worse through the Industrial Revolution of the 1800s, with air and water pollution becoming a major issue. Drinking water was contaminated as factories poured waste into streams, lakes, and rivers. People died from the poisonous smog that drifted over cities and towns. It was during this time that Henry David Thoreau moved to Walden Pond and began to write about the idea that humans are part of nature, and we function best when we remember that.

The late 1800s and early 1900s were a pivotal time for ecological awareness. People began demanding better air, land, and water quality. They began to call for a National Park System to enjoy with their families. Key leaders during this era played a vital role in elevating interest in conservationism. In 1866, the German botanist Ernst Haeckel coined the word *ecology* from the Greek *oikos*, which means "household," and *logos*, which means "to study." So, the term *ecology* means "the study of the household," with household referring to nature.

Conservation efforts began to take off in the 1800s. In 1864, President Abraham Lincoln signed a bill granting the Yosemite Valley and the Mariposa Grove of Giant Sequoias to the state of California as an inalienable public trust. This was followed in 1872 with Yellowstone becoming the nation's first National Park, and the establishment of Yosemite National Park in 1890. John Muir, a noted naturalist and conservationist, began to fight for the protection of other, untouched wilderness preserves across the nation. He founded the Sierra Club, an environmental organization, in 1892 to help fight for the protection of wilderness and to encourage responsible use of the earth's resources. Following these movements toward preservation and conservation, President Teddy Roosevelt created the U.S. Forest Service in 1906.

Numerous other environmental societies were formed during this time:

❂ The Audubon Society was founded in 1886.
❂ The National Park Service was founded in 1916.
❂ The Wilderness Society was founded in 1935.

In 1962, the book *Silent Spring,* written by Rachel Carson, alerted the public to the dangers of pesticides, sparking a newly refreshed attention to environmental issues. Other events, including governmental legislation, have fueled the rise in ecological awareness since the publication of Carson's book. These events include:

✿ In 1970, the Environmental Protection Agency was created.

✿ Also in 1970, the National Environmental Policy Act was passed, requiring federal agents to consider potential environmental impacts before taking action or funding programs..

✿ 1970 saw the passing of the Clean Air Act and the creation of Earth Day.

✿ The pesticide DDT was banned in 1972, and the Water Pollution Control Act was passed that same year.

✿ Since its passing in 1973, the Endangered Species Act has been one of the most influential acts in the control of the environment.

✿ More than 75% of Americans are self-proclaimed "environmentalists," according to a Gallup Poll conducted during the 1990s.

✿ Julia "Butterfly" Hill spent 2 years (1997–1999) in a 180-foot tall California Coast Redwood tree, coming down after reaching a deal with Pacific Lumber/Maxxam Corporation to save the tree and three surrounding acres of trees.

Today, the agencies created over the last century continue to work on advocacy, research, and development of solutions to ecological awareness and problems. The fight to save our Earth is ongoing.

Why Teach Ecology to Kids?

A study of ecology provides students with an interdisciplinary chance to investigate their environment. By allowing students to "get their hands dirty" and fully participate in a scientific study, a teacher can generate an excitement about the natural world that can translate into a lifelong ecological awareness and positive feelings toward conservationism. Children are naturally interested in the environment around them; they see plants and animals all the time and, from the time they begin to speak, try to understand how everything fits together. Teachers can capitalize on this interest and engage students in a project where they will explore all subject areas, including mathematics, science, language arts, social studies, fine arts, dramatic arts, and group dynamics, and not even know it.

There is a beauty in being still and becoming one with nature. Through the activities in this book, students will learn to be active observers, recording and processing the things going on around them, while appreciating the wonder of uncovering nature's secrets. Fieldwork, experiments, and learning to use scientific equipment is fascinating for young children, who are often capable of more than we give them credit for. Kids thrive on knowing what is expected of them and on finding consistency in their world. Why not consistently give them high standards for which to reach? They may surprise you. Children are amazingly capable of rising to whatever challenge you present.

How Can You Use This Book?

The primary goals in writing this book were to:

❁ offer teachers a guide for educating children about their environment and teaching them that they can have a real contribution to conservation;

❁ allow students a chance to experience a real, hands-on study in the field of environmental science;

❁ teach students about the fragile nature of our environment and give them an appreciation for the impact humans have;

❁ provide teachers with a road map of information to draw from as they guide their students on the road to discovery; and

❁ help raise an environmentally aware generation of citizens to help protect the planet's nonrenewable resources.

This book is set up in chapters that encompass lessons about the field of ecology. Following each narrative is a collection of activities with any reproducibles or forms you would need to complete that activity. The lessons are broken up with a reference to the activity or activities that best illustrate the principles being taught. Feel free to pick and choose the activities that best suit your class and situation. The most important thing in any unit of study is that a teacher makes it his or her own. You know your students best. Choose the activities that best teach the concepts you find important and those that will best engage your kids.

The appendix contains numerous resources you may find helpful to have on hand. Read through the lists and review the books, magazines, and Web sites at your leisure and determine which best fit your needs. Remember that this is your guide. Personalize it in anyway you wish. Choose topics within this study that interest you—after all, your engagement is important! Most of all, have fun with this book. A study of the environment can generate so much excitement in your students that you may be surprised by the depth of their knowledge and abilities. Engagement is a fabulous motivator for furthering student achievement.

Chapter 1

Preparing the Essentials

When beginning any new unit of study, you must be sure you have everything you need. Glance through this book and make a note of any special materials or preparation you will need before attempting the activities.

One of the most important decisions you will need to make is where to conduct the activities in this book. Scout around your school grounds for a location that does not get a lot of foot traffic, is secluded enough to be attractive to various wildlife, and available to use for an extended period of time, eventually transforming it into a wildlife garden. Talk with your principal, grounds crew, superintendent, or board of education, making sure you do what is needed to secure permission to dig, experiment, and create habitats on the grounds. You may want to contact your local PTA members and see if they would be interested in helping to fund your project, because you will be leaving behind a wonderful garden for others to enjoy.

Next, put together a resource library using the suggestions in the appendix. Gather as many books, magazines, videos, computer programs, games, and center activities related to the field of ecology as you can. When a child is surrounded by the topic he is to study using a variety of modalities, he can become more interested and motivated to achieve.

Choose resources from the lists in the appendix, but don't rely on them completely. This is your unit. Personalize it by choosing additional resources based on your interests and preferences. Use the appendix as a jumping off point—a means to point you in the right direction. Hold a few things back and pull them out from time to time to reinvigorate your students. A new game or Web site can go a long way toward keeping the excitement alive within the classroom.

Don't forget live resources! Find out who is working in the field of ecology or environmental sciences in your area. Contact local colleges and universities, parks, nature preserves, and the like. Ask if anyone is willing to come out and talk to your class or volunteer to help facilitate experiments or activities. Often, there are many untapped experts right around the corner. You never know who you'll discover when talking about your upcoming project.

Activity 1

AN ECOLOGY DICTIONARY

Subjects and Skills	Language arts, science, using reference materials
Rationale	This activity will introduce students to terms they will encounter throughout the activities, giving them prior knowledge from which to draw. This activity will also allow students to practice using guide words and choosing relevant definitions.
Objectives	The students will identify and define terms common to the field.
Activity Preparation	1. Discuss the importance of preparation before exploring a new field of study. 2. Teach or review with students the way to use a dictionary (using guide words, reading through definitions to find the one best suited for their purpose, etc.).
Activity Procedures	1. Sort students into pairs and provide each with a dictionary and the ecology dictionary handout. 2. Have each pair define terms, using their own words to facilitate understanding. 3. This dictionary will eventually go into students' field journals as a reference tool.
Materials Needed	pens or pencils dictionaries (one per pair of students) An Ecology Dictionary handout
Vocabulary	**guide words**—words found in the upper left- and righthand corners of the dictionary pages to help you locate the words found alphabetically within that page

An Ecology Dictionary

adaptation _____

_____

atmosphere_____

_____

carbon cycle _____

_____

carnivores_____

_____

climate _____

_____

community_____

_____

conservation_____

_____

consumers _____

_____

decay _____

_____

decomposers_____

_____

© Prufrock Press • *Hands-On Ecology*
This page may be photocopied or reproduced with permission for student use.

Name: _____ Date _____

decomposition _____

_____

diversity _____

_____

ecologist _____

_____

ecology_____

_____

ecosystem _____

_____

energy _____

_____

endangered species _____

_____

environment_____

_____

erosion _____

_____

evolution _____

_____

© Prufrock Press • *Hands-On Ecology*
This page may be photocopied or reproduced with permission for student use.

extinction _____

_____

food chain _____

_____

food web _____

_____

global warming _____

_____

greenhouse effect _____

_____

habitat _____

_____

herbivores _____

_____

omnivores _____

_____

ozone layer _____

_____

pesticides _____

_____

Name: _____ Date _____

pH _____

_____

photosynthesis _____

_____

pollution _____

_____

population _____

_____

predator _____

_____

prey _____

_____

producer _____

_____

recycling _____

_____

water cycle _____

_____

weathering _____

_____

Activity 2

CREATING A JOURNAL

Subjects and Skills	Language arts, science
Rationale	Keeping a field journal is a great way to get students used to making observations and recording them. Observing nature is engaging and a field journal will provide a means of ongoing assessment of the students' progress and understanding, as well as a tool for students' collections of handouts, vocabulary, and observations about the study.
Objectives	Students will keep a daily journal of observations, hypotheses, and conclusions throughout the study of ecology. They will also keep any paperwork encumbered as a result of an activity or experiment in this journal so everything related to this unit is in one place.
Activity Preparation	1. Discuss the importance of keeping a journal to document fieldwork. A scientist uses her journal to keep a permanent record of what is going on in the natural world—kind of like a diary of nature. It is a vehicle for looking back on observations to discover patterns. 2. Explain the function of a scientific journal: It serves as documentation of field observations, working hypotheses, questions, experiments, and activities, and houses sketches or photographs. 3. Share sample journals borrowed from the public library or local museums.
Activity Procedures	1. Have students create a cover for their journals. Be sure to have them include their name, grade, school, and title for their field study. You may want to have students design their own covers or use the worksheet provided. 2. Make sure each student has 10–15 sheets of blank notebook paper, a small three-hole pencil pouch, pencils, and other supplies inside their journals. 3. Take a nature walk and allow students time to make their first entry. Remind them of the importance of using description: All senses should be included in observations of the natural world—sight, smell, taste (if appropriate and safe), hearing, and touch. Encourage them to add sketches or illustrations. Some students may want to bring along colored pencils to add color to their drawings.
Materials Needed	sample field journal and scientists' notebooks (check out local libraries and universities)

three-ring binders
notebook paper
pencils
colored pencils
pencil pouches
A Field Study of Ecology reproducible cover page (optional)

Vocabulary   **field journal**—journals kept by scientists in the field to record their observations, gather information, keep track of questions, form new ideas, and sketch the things they see

observation—recognizing and noting some fact or occurrence in nature

sketch—a rough drawing

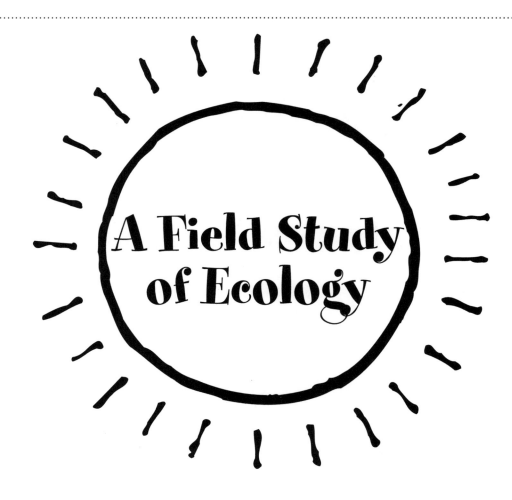

A Field Study of Ecology

Name: _____

Grade: _____

School: _____

Teacher: _____

Date: _____

© Prufrock Press • *Hands-On Ecology*
This page may be photocopied or reproduced with permission for student use.

Activity 3

BUILDING AN ECOLOGY TOOLKIT

Subjects and Skills	Science
Rationale	By preparing a toolkit in advance, you will build student excitement and motivation. You will also introduce the children to some of the activities they will be completing as you explain what each tool is used for.
Objectives	Students will collaborate to build a classroom toolkit, as well as smaller personal or group toolkits.
Activity Preparation	1. Collect the materials you will need to build a large classroom toolkit and several smaller personal or group toolkits. 2. Send a letter home to parents asking for material donations and help during your ecology unit.
Activity Procedures	1. Hold up items, one at a time, asking students to predict what they are used for. Explain their function and put them in the bin where they will be housed. 2. Follow the same procedure while organizing small student kits. Make sure you have at least one student kit for every 2–3 students.

Materials Needed	parent letter (see p. 17)
	large plastic bin for classroom kit
	small plastic toolboxes for student kits
	various tools:
	    stakes
	    hammers
	    measuring tapes
	    string
	    rain gauge
	    pH test strips
	    thermometers
	    rulers
	    hula hoops
	    trowels
	    binoculars
	    insect nets
	    Ziploc bags in various sizes

marking pens
large pie pans
tweezers
magnifying glasses (large and small)
microscopes
plastic slides
index cards
double stick tape
test tubes
small plastic aquariums
field guides to:
   insects
   trees
   flowering plants
   ferns
   mosses
   mushrooms
   birds
   mammals
   reptiles
   amphibians
clipboards
cameras
film

Vocabulary   **field guide**—a book used to identify species of plants, animals, or fungi

Dear Parents:

   As we begin our study of ecology, we will prepare toolkits to use to conduct experiments and activities. If you have any of these objects (or anything else you think will be helpful to our study), and are able to donate them to our classroom, please send them in with your child.

- ✿ Wooden stakes
- ✿ Hammers
- ✿ Measuring tapes
- ✿ String or twine
- ✿ Thermometers
- ✿ Hula hoops
- ✿ Trowels and other gardening tools
- ✿ Binoculars
- ✿ Insect nets
- ✿ Various sized Ziploc bags
- ✿ Aluminum pie tins
- ✿ Small plastic aquariums
- ✿ Plastic 2-liter bottles with the labels removed
- ✿ Various local field guides for plants, animals, and fungi

   If you are available to donate your time during any part of this unit, we could use extra hands for several of the activities. Please complete the bottom portion of this form and send it in with your child.

   Thank you for your consideration of these requests.

Sincerely,

_____

- -

I would like to help out during this unit.

I am available on the following mornings:
M   T   W   Th   F

I am available on the following afternoons:
M   T   W   Th   F

My name is _____

My child's name is _____

My phone number is _____

Activity 4

INTERVIEWING A NATURALIST

Subjects and Skills	Social studies, science, language arts
Rationale	This activity provides students with an opportunity to discover who is working in the field of ecology in their area, to compile a list of these people as resources, and to find out about the important aspects of their jobs.
Objectives	Students will use local resource guides to create a list of naturalists and ecologists working in their area. They will use oral language skills to interview and gather information about those working in the field.

Activity Preparation

1. Discuss some different jobs in the field and the responsibility of each.

Activity Procedures

1. Brainstorm a list of important things to find out about the various ecological jobs and the people performing them.
2. Use the resource guides to choose possible contacts and compile these contacts and their information into a local directory to be included in the students' field journals.
3. E-mail or call these chosen contacts to request a phone or e-mail interview with your students.
4. Have students interview their contacts and take detailed notes of their interviews. You will want them to write out their questions ahead of time for you to check for accuracy, relevance, etc. You should also have your students practice for their interview with you or a partner. This will teach them interviewing skills and help ease any nervousness about the interviews.

Materials Needed

pencils and paper
telephone directories
faculty lists from local universities
computers with Internet access
A Local Directory of the Ecology Field handout

Vocabulary

naturalist—a person who studies the natural world and natural history
ecologist—a scientist who studies the field of ecology

Name: _____ Date _____

A Local Directory of the Ecology Field

Compiled _____ (date)

Job title	Name	Affiliation	Address	Web site	Phone number	E-mail address

Activity 5

A DAY IN THE LIFE OF AN ECOLOGIST

Subjects and Skills	Science, language arts, dramatic arts
Rationale	By role-playing ecology jobs, students will gain an appreciation and understanding of the responsibilities involved in working in the field.
Objectives	Students will synthesize information gathered from their interviews with scientists and create a skit about "A Day in the Life . . ."
Activity Preparation	1. Discuss qualities of good scripts—believable dialogue and action. 2. Break students into small groups.
Activity Procedures	1. Have small groups of students work together to write scripts, based on their interview information, that detail a day in the life of a scientist. 2. Allow them time for peer editing and rehearsal over the course of several days. 3. Have a performance day—each small group will perform their skits for the rest of the class. For added meaning and fun, invite the principal and/or younger classes to be a part of the audience. Or, host a "Drama Night" and invite parents to attend.
Materials Needed	paper pencils costumes and props
Vocabulary	**script**—the text of a play or other act of drama **dialogue**—the words spoken by characters

Chapter

What Is an Ecosystem?

Defining the Term

In 1935, the British Botanist Arthur Tansley created the term *ecosystem* to describe the communities of organisms interacting with one another. During the late 1800s and early 1900s, he was instrumental in leading the movement toward conservationism by using sampling methods to study ecological patterns and to facilitate understanding of the impact humans have on their environment. Understanding what makes an ecosystem and what role humans play in their ecosystem is essential to a study of ecological science.

An ecosystem is made up of living things interacting with one another and the nonliving things within their habitat. Their composition and structure can be defined by several environmental factors like nutrient availability, water sources, plant growth and life, and temperature. Anytime changes occur in these factors, the structure of the ecosystem is affected. For example, a forest fire flattens and kills life in an area once populated with old, large trees. Mosses, shrubs, and other organisms are killed and their nutrients are released into the atmosphere. After a time, a new ecosystem of grasses and seedlings replaces the formerly well-established forest area. Ecosystems vary in size—they can be as large as an ocean (and bigger), or as small a tide pool. A tree, the muddy area beneath a rock, and the planet Earth—these are all separate, but interconnected, ecosystems.

Interdependence

Organisms depend on their ecosystems for survival. The community in which they live provides everything they require for survival. Food, water, shelter, light, protection, and nutrients are all necessary for an organism to thrive. How can humans impact the balance and the provisions found within various ecosystems around them? How can they provide for the specific needs of plants and animals within their care and what can they learn from these lessons? Students will learn more about interdependence in Activities 6 and 11.

One of the most important factors in an organism's survival is what it needs to make energy. Plants make their own food by using a process called photosynthesis. Photosynthesis is the process plants have of converting light energy from the sun into a carbohydrate and storing it for its own use.

This process takes place in the chloroplasts usually found in the leaves of a plant using its chlorophyll, the pigment that makes plants green. A plant takes in water from the ground through its roots, and splits it into hydrogen and oxygen using the energy the chlorophyll absorbs from the sun. The hydrogen mixes with carbon dioxide from the air to make the sugar a plant needs for food. This sugar is carried to other parts in the plant, the leftover oxygen is released into the air, and the process begins again. Activity 7 shows students how plants produce and use energy.

Animals, organisms that cannot make their own food, depend on their environment to provide what they need. Some animals are herbivores, eating only plant material found within their ecosystem. Others are carnivores, hunting their prey and feeding off their meat. Some organisms are omnivores and eat both plants and animals. Regardless of what they eat, all organisms are interdependent and form part of one or several food chains that can be connected to form larger food webs.

A food chain shows the connections between the eating habits of animals. For example, a simple forest food chain would show grass receiving its energy from the sun, a grasshopper feeding on the grass, a toad eating the grasshopper, a snake eating the toad, a hawk eating the snake, and bacteria breaking down the hawk's body into organic material after its death. All things can eventually be reduced to some kind of decomposer.

A food web is formed when several chains are put together to form a more complicated interdependence. Using the same web described above as a starting point, we can branch off and have the grasshopper eaten by a lizard, which is eaten by an eagle, or we can show the grasshopper eaten by a bird, and so on. Students will learn about food chains and webs in Activity 8.

When plants and animals die, they are eaten by decomposers like fungi, worms, and bacteria. These organisms break down dead materials into chemical parts. Nitrogen, carbon, and other nutrients can then be used again by plants and animals. Decomposition is essential to an ecosystem's survival because without it, dead plants and animals would simply rot and the environment would become contaminated and inhabitable.

Mildew, fungus, and insects assist in the decomposition of plants and animals. Scavenger insects also break down dead organisms by eating and tunneling through them. These insects become food for other creatures in the woods.

Mildew and bacteria help break down the organisms once scavengers are finished feeding off the carcasses. All decomposers break down or cause organic matter to rot. This returns them to the soil and earth. Some of our best topsoil is in the woods, because of the abundance of decomposers. Activities 9 and 10 will teach students more about decomposers and decomposition.

Activity 6

PROVIDING THE ESSENTIALS

Subjects and Skills	Science, language arts
Rationale	This activity will help students gain an understanding that all organisms rely on their environments for essential elements of survival.
Objectives	Students will learn what all organisms need in order to survive. Students will understand that a complete ecosystem provides everything the organisms contained within need to survive.
Activity Preparation	1. Purchase or borrow a small potted plant and a small animal for this activity. (You may want to keep both as new additions to your classroom community. This would provide a nice opportunity for ongoing observations about the needs of organisms. Gerbils, guinea pigs, lizards, frogs, or hermit crabs all make nice classroom pets—be sure to check your school's policy about keeping plants and animals in the classroom.) 2. Discuss with students the reliance that all organisms have on their environments. They count on their habitat to provide food, shelter, water, and light in order to survive.
Activity Procedures	1. Show the plant and the animal to the students. 2. Facilitate a discussion and brainstorming session about each organism's needs. 3. Have students record each organism's basic needs and sketch the ideal habitat for each on the worksheet on p. 26. 4. Following this brainstorming, have students assist in building the cage setup if you will be keeping the animal as a class pet.

Materials Needed	small potted plant
	small animal (e.g., gerbils, guinea pig, rat, turtle)
	appropriate cage and supplies:
	    bedding
	    water bowl or bottle
	    food bowl
	    food
	pencils

Providing the Essentials for Our Class Pet worksheet
field journals

Vocabulary **organism**—a living thing
habitat—a plant where a plant or animal naturally lives

What Is an Ecosystem?

Name: _____ Date _____

Providing the Essentials
for Our Class Pet

In the box below, illustrate your organism's ideal habitat.

What are your organism's food and shelter needs?

_____

_____

_____

Describe how you would set up the ideal habitat or cage for our class pet. Be sure to keep in mind its food and shelter needs!

_____

_____

_____

_____

_____

© Prufrock Press • *Hands-On Ecology*
This page may be photocopied or reproduced with permission for student use.

Name: _____ Date _____

Providing the Essentials
for Our Class Plant

In the box below, illustrate your plant's ideal habitat.

What are your plant's food, water, light, and shelter needs?

_____

_____

_____

Describe how you would set up the ideal habitat for our class plant. Be sure to keep in mind its food, water, light, and shelter needs!

_____

_____

_____

_____

_____

Activity 7

PRODUCING NATURE'S ENERGY

Subjects and Skills
Science, group dynamics

Rationale
This activity facilitates student understanding of photosynthesis and the transfer of energy within the natural world.

Objectives
Students will understand the hierarchy of energy transfer and the important role producers perform.

Students will know that without sunlight a plant cannot use the process of photosynthesis.

Activity Preparation
1. Discuss photosynthesis, the ability of plants to produce organic material from inorganic, and the transfer of energy between producers and consumers.
2. Go over the Energy Hierarchy/Pyramid Chart so students understand the relationship between producers and consumers.
3. Brainstorm a list of producers and consumers found around the schoolyard.

Activity Procedures
1. Divide students into small groups, each with a leafy potted plant and tag board.
2. Have students cut out simple shapes from the tag board (e.g., circles, squares, stars, hearts, sunbursts).
3. Ask students to paperclip each shape on a different leaf of the plant, covering half of the leaf with the tag board.
4. Once students have clipped several shapes to the leaves of their plant, choose a sunny window in which to place the plants.
5. Over the next 2 weeks, have students record notes about the weather on their recording sheets.
6. Following the 2-week observation period, have students work in their same small groups to remove their tag board shapes and compare the covered parts of the leaves with the uncovered parts.
7. Ask them to write their observations on their recording sheets and answer the discussion questions.

Materials Needed
several small potted plants with large, leafy leaves (pothos work well)
tag board
paperclips
pencils

paper
field journal
Energy Hierarchy/Pyramid Chart
Producing Nature's Energy Observation Record worksheet

Vocabulary   **producer**—an organism that can create its own organic compound
consumer—an organism that feeds on other organisms
photosynthesis—when plants form carbohydrates from carbon dioxide and water
organic—made up of or related to living organisms
inorganic—being composed of material that is not derived from plant or animal matter
chlorophyll—green pigments in a plant that aid in photosynthesis
energy—usable power
herbivore—a plant-eating animal
carnivore—a flesh-eating animal
omnivore—an animal that eats both plants and animals

Energy Hierarchy/Pyramid Chart

© Prufrock Press • *Hands-On Ecology*
This page may be photocopied or reproduced with permission for student use.

Name: _____ Date _____

Producing Nature's Energy Observation Record

Procedures

1. With your partners, cut out small simple shapes from the tag board provided (e.g., circles, squares, stars, hearts, sunbursts).
2. Paperclip each shape on a different leaf of the plant, covering half of the leaf with the tag board.
3. Choose a sunny window in which to place the plants.
4. What do you think will happen to the part of the leaf that is covered? Write your hypothesis on the lines provided below.
5. Over the next 2 weeks, record notes about the weather in the observation chart.
6. When 2 weeks have passed, remove your tag board shapes and compare the covered parts of the leaves with the uncovered parts.
7. Write your observations in the space provided and answer the discussion questions.

What is your hypothesis? _____

_____

_____

_____

Conclusion

What does your plant look like? Why do you think this happened?

_____

_____

_____

Name: _____ Date _____

When keeping houseplants at home, where should you place them? Why?

_____

_____

_____

Where have you seen these effects in nature?

_____

_____

_____

Where would you expect to find fewer plants outside? Why?

_____

_____

_____

© Prufrock Press • *Hands-On Ecology*

32   This page may be photocopied or reproduced with permission for student use.

Name: _____ Date _____

Observation Chart	
Date	**Weather Conditions**

© Prufrock Press • *Hands-On Ecology*
This page may be photocopied or reproduced with permission for student use.

Activity 8

FOOD WEB

Subjects and Skills	Science, art, language arts
Rationale	It is important to note the interdependence of organisms.
Objectives	Students will create a food web poster to demonstrate the interdependence of organisms within their local ecosystem.
Activity Preparation	1. Discuss roles of various participants in food chains. Plants (producers) use the sun's energy (photosynthesis) to make food, and sunlight turns molecules of water and carbon dioxide gas into sugar inside a leaf. Herbivores (consumers) eat plants, carnivores (also consumers) eat herbivores, and when carnivores die, decomposers break down their bodies into enriched soil, helping plants to grow. You may want to have some sample diagrams of food chains and webs available for students to observe. 2. Brainstorm different producers, consumers, and decomposers found in the general area of the school.
Activity Procedures	1. Have students find and cut out pictures of the different organisms they brainstormed by using old magazines. Or, students could draw and cut out these organisms. They will also need a picture of the sun. 2. Using these pictures, create a food web showing who eats what. 3. Using a large piece of poster board, spread out the sun and organisms. 4. Once they are laid out on the board, glue them in place and connect them to each other with yarn or ribbon. Use yellow ribbon to connect producers to the sun, use green ribbon to connect herbivores to the plants, use red ribbon to connect carnivores to the herbivores, and use blue ribbon to connect the decomposers to the animals and plants they break down into soil after they die. 5. Observe how everything in an ecosystem is interconnected. 6. Have students write about their observations in their field journal or on the Food Webs handout provided on p. 35.
Materials Needed	magazines scissors glue poster board various colored ribbon or yarn field journal

Food Webs handout
pencils

Vocabulary **food chain**—an arrangement of organisms according to what they eat and what eats them
food web—the interaction of multiple food chains
decomposition—the decay of an organism
decay—to decompose

Name: _____   Date _____

Food Webs

1. Draw a small sketch of your food web in the box below.

2. What organisms did you include in your food web? Label them.

_____

_____

_____

3. What did you notice about how they connect to each other?

_____

_____

_____

4. Imagine that one of the animals you included on your web were to die out from the area you live. What would happen to the other organisms involved in that food web?

_____

_____

_____

5. What could the other organisms in your area do to adapt to the absence of this organism?

_____

_____

_____

6. What if a plant you included died out? How would that affect the herbivores that feed off of the plant?

_____

_____

_____

7. Would it affect the carnivores too? How?

_____

_____

_____

Activity 9

DECOMPOSITION

Subjects and Skills	Science
Rationale	This activity will help students understand the importance of decomposers and the role they play in the environment.
Objectives	The students will observe decomposers at work over the period of several days, making regular observations and revising hypotheses.
Activity Preparation	1. Discuss the role of decomposers in nature—to break down dead material and waste matter until chemicals can be released into the air, soil, and water, making them available to other living things. 2. Gather the materials needed for the experiment.
Activity Procedures	1. Ask students to form a hypothesis as to what will happen to each small piece of food, how long it will take, and what the food will look like as it decomposes. Students should write these hypotheses in their journals. 2. Set up the experiments in small groups. 3. Place pieces of food into small, clear boxes or jars. 4. Add a few drops of water to each item and place the lid on the box or jar. 5. Place the box in a cool area where it is easily observed. (After a few days, mold, bacteria, and other fungi will begin to grow. Mold often will produce tiny black spores—this is how molds reproduce.) 6. Continue watching over the course of several days or weeks. Have the students make daily observations, including illustrations, of what is happening in their student field journals. *Note:* Be careful not to breathe in the mold spores or get them into your mouth. Students should always observe the molds while lids are in place.
Materials Needed	field journals Decomposition Experiment handout pencils colored pencils pieces of bread, tomato, apples, crackers, or other fruits or vegetables clear plastic boxes with lids or clear mason or mayonnaise jars with lids water and droppers

Vocabulary **decomposer**—an organism that feeds on and breaks down the dead

mold—a fuzzy growth, a fungus

bacteria—single-celled life forms that can reproduce quickly

fungi—a group of organisms that lack chlorophyll and obtain nutrients from dead or living plants or animals

spores—seeds of mold or fungi

What Is an Ecosystem?

Decomposition Experiment

Set up your experiment:

1. Place pieces of food into small, clear boxes or jars.
2. Add a few drops of water to each item and place the lid on the box or jar tightly.
3. Place the box in a cool area where you can watch it easily.
4. Continue watching for the time you teacher has determined. Make daily observations, including illustrations, of what is happening on this page. Keep it in your journal.

Be careful not to breathe in the mold spores or get them into your mouth! You should always observe this experiment while the lids are in place.

Determine your hypothesis:
What do you think will happen to the food in the jars?

_____

_____

_____

_____

Observations:
Record your observations in the Decomposition Observation Chart.

Conclusions:
1. What happened to the food in the jars?

_____

_____

_____

_____

© Prufrock Press • *Hands-On Ecology*
This page may be photocopied or reproduced with permission for student use.

2. Why do you think this happened?

_____

_____

_____

_____

3. Do you think moistening the food with water contributes to its decomposition? Why or why not?

_____

_____

_____

_____

4. How could you design this experiment differently to find out if moisture is important?

_____

_____

_____

_____

Name: _____ Date _____

Decomposition Observation Chart	
Date	**What I Saw**

© Prufrock Press • *Hands-On Ecology*
This page may be photocopied or reproduced with permission for student use.

Activity 10

WORM HABITAT

Subjects and Skills	Science, language arts, group dynamics
Rationale	This activity will help students appreciate the value of worms and the benefits they provide to nature. They will also have the opportunity to view decomposers at work.
Objectives	Students will build a habitat for worms and record their observations.
Activity Preparation	1. Send letter requesting supplies home with students. 2. Discuss a worm's role in nature, relating it back to the decomposition experiment. 3. Solicit parent helpers for the activity date. 4. Using an Exacto knife, cut off the top portion of the 2-liter bottles. The teacher should cut the bottles **before** the day of the activity.
Activity Procedures	1. Pass out and go over the information sheet, describing how to set up the habitat. Make sure to clarify any questions the students might have. 2. Split students into small groups to create habitats together. Have a parent volunteer assigned to each group so you can walk around, facilitating the disbursement of supplies, answering questions, and providing guidance. 3. Have students record their initial observations of the worms' behavior after placing them into their new habitats, then cover the bottles up with a cloth or dark paper, so the worms are in the dark. (If the worms are in the dark, they will build their tunnels and burrows against the walls of the bottles for easy observations.) 4. As students observe their habitats each day, have them use tracing paper to trace the pattern of tunnels the worms have created. You will need to remove the dark paper or cloth for the tracings, but be sure to replace them when the observations are complete each day. They should date these drawings and include them in their field journals. *Note:* While you will only need to make observations for a week, have your students maintain the habitats until the worms are needed for your composting activity (Activity 34), then they can harvest them to add to the compost bin.
Materials Needed	field journals pencils tracing paper Building a Worm Habitat handout

Building a Worm Habitat Observation Form handout
unit of worms (available from science supply catalogues)
clean 2-liter soda bottles with the labels taken off
plastic wrap
rubber bands
spray bottles
dark cloths
unfertilized potting soil
dead leaves
food scraps (fruits and vegetables only—meat will rot and smell)
rocks or gravel
cornmeal
parent letter

Vocabulary
burrow—to move through the ground by digging
topsoil—the rich upper layer of soil, from which plants get most of their nutrients
worm castings—worm excrement, containing rich nutrients

Dear Parents,

We will be building worm habitats soon so we can observe these amazing decomposers at work and we need your help. Our worms will be living in habitats made out of clean 2-liter bottles. Please send in your washed bottles with the labels removed as soon as you can.

If you have any of the other supplies listed below, please send them in, as well. We can use whatever you have to offer!

- ❁ Plastic wrap
- ❁ Spray bottles for misting habitats with water
- ❁ Unfertilized potting soil
- ❁ Small rocks or gravel

Please send in your supply of donations with your child by _____.

If you are able to help assemble our habitats on _____, send in the bottom portion of this note and I will call you to coordinate the schedule.

Thank you for any help you are able to provide.

Sincerely,

_____

- -

I can help set up worm habitats!

Name: _____

Phone Number: _____

Name: _____ Date _____

Building a Worm Habitat

1. Place a layer of rocks or gravel on the bottom of your 2-liter bottle.

2. Add a layer of soil on top of the rocks.

3. For your final layer, mix cornmeal, leaves, and any food scraps your teacher has collected and put on this top of the soil.

4. Lightly spray the habitat with your spray bottle—do not soak it—and add two to four worms to the top.

5. Secure plastic wrap on the top, poking several holes for air to get in.

6. Sketch your habitat on your observation record and put the paper in your field journal to record the changes each day.

7. Finally, cover the sides of your habitat with a dark cloth or paper and put it in a cool, dark place.

© Prufrock Press • Hands-On Ecology

This page may be photocopied or reproduced with permission for student use.

Name: _____ Date _____

Building a Worm Habitat Observation Form

Once you have set up your habitat, sketch it in the box below and describe the behavior of your worms on the lines below the box.

```

```

_____

_____

_____

Each day for the next week:

1. Remove the cloth or paper from the outside of your worm habitat.
2. Tape tracing paper to your bottle and trace the different layers and any tunnels your worms have made.
3. Make observations below your drawing describing the behavior of your worms when you removed the cloth.
4. Take your worms out of their habitat and measure them. Record their measurements on the bottom of your tracing paper. Try not to disturb your habitat when you take out the worms.
5. Put your worms back in the bottle, sprinkle some more cornmeal on top and lightly spritz the habitat with water from your spray bottle, then cover it up again, and put it back in the safe place you are keeping it.
6. Keep your tracing paper records in your field journal. Make sure you date each page.

© Prufrock Press • *Hands-On Ecology*
This page may be photocopied or reproduced with permission for student use.

Activity 11

CREATING MINI-ECOSYSTEMS

Subjects and Skills	Science, language arts, group dynamics, public speaking

Rationale — By creating and observing small versions of the various ecosystems, students will gain an appreciation for what it takes to sustain each.

Objectives — Students will build a mini-ecosystem to serve as a vehicle for ongoing observation.

Activity Preparation

1. Solicit parent help for this activity.
2. Prior to this activity, discuss with students the different ecosystems being made and have students fill out ballots showing which they would like to work on. Use these ballots to create small groups of students, trying to give each child either their first or second choice of ecosystem.
3. Decide whether you want all students to observe each type of ecosystem each day or just the one they created and choose the appropriate observation form handout.

Activity Procedures

1. Assign each small group to a parent helper and distribute materials and instruction sheets. Have each group follow the procedures on the instruction sheet, creating the mini-ecosystem.
2. Each small group should share its finished project with the class, explaining what went into each and how the living things depend on one another for survival. (So students don't have to bring their ecosystems to the front of the room, this could be done in "museum style," where the class goes from "exhibit" to "exhibit," standing in a large circle around it while the group shares.)
3. Students could use this time to make their first observation of each ecosystem on their observation form.

Materials Needed — ballots
Mini-Ecosystem Observation Record worksheet
Mini-Ecosystem project sheets
materials specific to the types of ecosystems you will be creating
plastic aquariums or other suitable containers

Vocabulary — **ecosystem**—a community of organisms and its environment
environment—the circumstances and conditions that surround and influence an organism
substrate—the surface on which an organism grows

Name: _____

First Choice: _____

Second Choice: _____

Least Favorite: _____

Name: _____

First Choice: _____

Second Choice: _____

Least Favorite: _____

Name: _____

First Choice: _____

Second Choice: _____

Least Favorite: _____

Name: _____

First Choice: _____

Second Choice: _____

Least Favorite: _____

Name: _____ Date _____

Mini-Ecosystems Observation Record

Observe your ecosystem for 5–10 minutes each day and write and illustrate what is happening.

Day of Observation:_____

What's happening in your ecosystem? Write about it.

_____

_____

_____

_____

Draw a picture showing what's happening in your ecosystem:

What care have you given to your animal since your last illustration?

_____

_____

_____

© Prufrock Press • *Hands-On Ecology*
This page may be photocopied or reproduced with permission for student use.

Name: _____ Date _____

Answer the following questions:

1. What are the living things in your ecosystem?

_____

_____

2. What are the nonliving things in your ecosystem?

_____

_____

3. Describe the changes that took place during your observation period.

_____

_____

_____

4. Describe the ways your organisms interacted with the other living things within the habitat.

_____

_____

_____

5. Describe the ways your organisms interacted with the nonliving things in your ecosystem.

_____

_____

_____

Name: _____ Date _____

Building a Mini-Pond Habitat

Ponds are wonderful habitats to explore. They can be found all over the world—in the city, the country, and the suburbs. You probably have one nearby or remember visiting one recently. Any pond, a small to medium body of water, can be home to many exciting plants and animals.

Most ponds have sandy or gravelly bottoms that help to establish plants and provide burrowing areas for turtles, bullfrogs, or other animals. Ponds teem with life. Water animals like tadpoles (which will become toads and frogs), fish, crayfish, newts, and turtles live happily in the depths and shallows, hunting or munching on algae and other plants. Heron, ducks, deer, beaver, and geese visit the area to feed, drink, and lay their eggs. Insects like damselflies and pond skaters zip through the air and skip around on the surface of the water.

Although it is exciting to visit and observe this habitat, it can be even more satisfying to create your own. A rough mix of sand and soil provides a solid substrate to anchor your plants and provide shelter for burrowing animals. By topping your sand and soil mix with gravel, stones, and sticks, your animals will have plenty of hiding places. Large rocks and stones that rise out of the water in the middle or on one side are important for frogs and newts, which need to be able to get out of the water from time to time to rest.

As important as animals are to a habitat, plants are even more crucial. Plants produce their own energy and release oxygen into the water so your animals can breathe and your water does not become stagnant. Plants also provide food for many of your inhabitants. Have fun building your mini-pond and observing your healthy habitat!

Materials Needed

❧ Elodea
❧ Duckweed
❧ Guppies
❧ Snails
❧ Tadpoles
❧ Newts

❧ Water insects
❧ Aquarium gravel
❧ Sticks
❧ Stones
❧ Sand
❧ Soil

❧ Pond water or tap water that has sat out for several days
❧ Aquarium or other container to house the habitat

© Prufrock Press • Hands-On Ecology
This page may be photocopied or reproduced with permission for student use.

Name: _____ Date _____

Procedures

1. Mix the sand and soil together and layer about ¼ inch on the bottom of the container.
2. Add about ½-inch layer of gravel, sticks, and stones.
3. Add the water slowly so you don't disturb the layers you just put in the bottom.
4. Put the duckweed, elodea, or any other water plants you found in the water—some plants will need to be anchored in the substrate (bottom); others just get sprinkled on top.
5. Introduce your animals to their new home. If you added newts or tadpoles, you will also need a large rock for the newts and frogs to pull themselves up out of the water.
6. Share your new habitat with your classmates. Observe what happens in your ecosystem as time passes.

Name: _____ Date _____

Building a Mini-Woodland Habitat

Woodland habitats are made up of lots of trees and bushes. There are shady areas with patchy sun peeking through the canopy of leaves overhead. Temperatures are usually moderate, ranging from just below freezing in the wintertime to the mid- to upper-80s in the summertime. The animals found in this habitat are diverse and have developed unique ways to adapt to the environments in which they live. From the teeny-tiny ant, to the imposing black bear, there are so many different creatures that can be found crawling over leaves and hiding in burrows.

The soil in a woodland habitat stays pretty moist, so it is important to add sand, gravel, and charcoal to a mini-habitat to prevent your soil from becoming sour and moldy. Woodland plants have an interesting life cycle. They bloom early in the spring, leaving only greenery by mid- to late summer. These plants have adapted to blooming early, to take advantage of the time period before the thick, leafy canopy blocks the sun.

Toads and salamanders take advantage of the leafy cover and moist soil for protection. They have readily available places to hide and a soft substrate for burrowing. Because the animals you will include in this habitat are carnivorous, you will need to provide them with a food source like crickets or mealworms, and a fresh source of water. Enjoy your observations! This is a fascinating world to discover.

Materials Needed

- Mosses
- Ferns
- Virginia Creepers
- Violets
- Primrose
- Any other easy to care for woodland plant
- Toad
- Salamander
- Pebbles

- Charcoal
- Sand
- Soil
- Stick pile or other hiding place for the animals
- Water dish
- Crickets (food source)
- Aquarium or other container to house the habitat

© Prufrock Press • *Hands-On Ecology*

54   This page may be photocopied or reproduced with permission for student use.

Procedures

1. Layer the sand, pebbles, and charcoal in the bottom ½ inch of your container.
2. Top with 1 inch of soil.
3. Plant your plants in the soil.
4. Add a water dish—partially buried—large enough for the toad and salamander to submerge half of their bodies in the water.
5. Set up the pile of sticks or other hiding place for the animals in a corner of your habitat.
6. Introduce your animals gently to their new home.
7. Wait a day before you offer them their food source, and then give them a few crickets each day (as much as they can eat in 15 minutes).
8. Share your habitat with your classmates. Observe what happens in your ecosystem as time passes.

Name: _____ Date _____

Building a Mini-Desert Habitat

Deserts are among the most difficult habitats in the world in which to survive because of their extreme heat and lack of moisture, but they contain some of the planet's most intriguing plants and animals. Deserts reach temperatures of more than 100 degrees during the day, yet they can get to the freezing point at night. Because their sandy and gravelly substrate is so barren, there is nothing to keep the sun from making the atmosphere too hot, and nothing to hold the warmth from the day near the ground when the sun goes down.

Desert animals have evolved to handle extremes. Most of them can survive on very little water and can absorb most of what their body needs needs from the foods that they eat. Many are nocturnal, which means they sleep and conserve energy during the day and come out at night when it is cooler. Some are crepuscular, which means that they are most active at twilight—both dawn and dusk—before it has gotten too hot or too cold.

The plants in a desert have adapted to their environment in unique ways, too. Many have long, deep roots that reach far below the surface to where water can be found. Some bloom for a short time following a heavy rain and then lie dormant until the next rain. Still others have interesting methods of storing water like the Saguaro cactus, whose outer pulp can expand like an accordion, helping it to save tons of water.

When keeping desert animals in your mini-habitat, it is important to help recreate the conditions of the desert in which they are found. You will need to provide a heat lamp to raise the daytime temperature of the habitat, as well as a heat mat that can be placed beneath your tank to keep one side of your habitat warmer to allow the animals to regulate their own body temperatures. Be sure to consult a care sheet or guide about the animals you will be housing before setting up your habitat, as you want to be sure their needs will be provided for.

Materials Needed

✿ Sand
✿ Soil
✿ Gravel

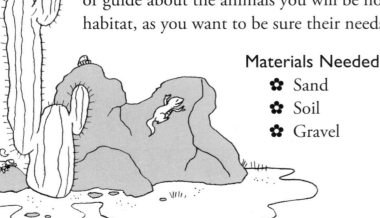

© Prufrock Press • *Hands-On Ecology*
This page may be photocopied or reproduced with permission for student use.

Materials Needed, continued

❁ Hardy desert plants—ask your local garden center about these. If you want animals in this ecosystem, you need to get nonprickly plants. If you choose not to have any animals, you could get a variety of cactus plants.

❁ Desert toad, leopard gecko, horned lizard, or tortoise

❁ Book on the care of the animals you have chosen

❁ Heat mat (if needed for your chosen animals)

❁ Heat lamp (if needed for your chosen animals)

❁ Water dish

❁ Crickets (food source)

❁ Aquarium or other suitable container to house the habitat

Procedures

1. Mix the soil and gravel in the bottom ¼ inch of the container.
2. Plant your chosen plants.
3. Place a thin layer of sand on top of the soil mixture.
4. Add water dish.
5. Introduce animals to their new habitat.
6. After they have acclimated themselves for a day or two, give them several crickets to eat.
7. Share your habitat with your classmates. Observe what happens in your ecosystem as time passes.

Building a Mini-Rainforest Habitat

A tropical rainforest is among the most fascinating places on Earth. There is an amazing interdependence between its plants and animals that makes it unique and self-sufficient, yet vulnerable. Because organisms rely on each other in such an integral way, rainforests have a difficult time adapting quickly. Each species much adapt to compensate for single changes—a difficult and sometimes impossible task.

Because the climate of the rainforest is hot and wet, with more than 80 inches of rainfall each year, plants have adaptations that allow them to shed excess water quickly and keep them safely in the ground in areas where soil could be displaced. Many have tips on their leaves that create a dripping effect and others have sturdy roots to hold tight to the moist, spongy soil and not get washed away. Plants have also evolved ways of taking in the little sunlight which makes its way through the thick canopy layer to the bottom of the rainforest floor. Large leaves help plants absorb as much sunlight as possible and some grow tall and thin, penetrating the canopy so they can reach the sunlight on their own.

Animals of the rainforest have amazing adaptations, too. Some, like the anole and other lizards, can climb trees and leaves searching for sunlight to bask in, raising their body temperatures, as they are cold-blooded. Poison dart frogs carry a lethal poison on their skin, killing many predators that try to eat them. Finally, toucans have four-toed feet, allowing them to hop from tree to tree, harvesting the fruit they eat and scattering seeds throughout the forest to help start new fruit trees.

Rainforests are amazing habitats, with many lessons to offer the observer. Make sure you read books about the care of anoles if you are adding this lizard to your habitat. Carefully recreate its habitat, complete with a basking lamp so it can keep its body temperature regulated.

Materials Needed

- Soil
- Charcoal
- Gravel
- Mosses
- Ferns
- Orchids
- African violets
- Anole lizard
- Small insects (food source)
- Basking lamp
- Book on anole lizard care
- Aquarium or other suitable container to house the habitat

© Prufrock Press • *Hands-On Ecology*
This page may be photocopied or reproduced with permission for student use.

Procedures

1. Mix ¼-inch of charcoal and gravel together on the bottom of your container.
2. Put a ¼-inch layer of soil on top of the gravel mixture.
3. Moisten soil and add plants to the terrarium.
4. Introduce your lizard to its new home and set the basking light on top of the setup.
5. Feed your anole regularly.
6. Share your habitat with your classmates. Observe what happens in your ecosystem as time passes.

Chapter

A Local Ecosystem

What neighbors do you have? What rivers, streams, ponds, forests, meadows, and other ecological features are in your area? Exploring the land around them will make this study personal and applicable for your students. This is the point where they can get down and dirty. Introduce you children to the observation site you have chosen to explore.

Nature can be tricky; what looks calm and peaceful can hide incredible activity and production: As students quietly observe a silent and still bird, suddenly it swoops and drags a worm out of the moist earth, while under the seemingly still water of a pond, a fish swims quietly but rapidly through the water. Giving kids a chance to learn about their environment allows them to take conservation to heart. Learning about the land in which they spend their days will give them new insight and appreciation for what they have. Activity 12 will help your students learn more about their area's ecology.

As students learned in the last section, ecosystems are filled with interactions between living things and their environment and interactions of living things with other living things. There are also many smaller ecosystems within larger ones. While conducting field observations, pay special attention to all of the ways organisms cooperate. Activity 13 looks at the interaction of ecosystems within ecosystems.

Your study site does not have to be large, but it should be diverse. Plants and animals should be present in it. A small section of meadow behind the art room, a tree-lined area across from the parking lot, or an unmowed section of grass and creek down the road are all possibilities. Be sure to check the area before introducing students, removing anything that could cause harm, like uneven areas that would make walking difficult, poison ivy, brambles, and thorny bushes and plants.

Now is the time to pull out all of those local field guides you have collected. Add some binoculars and magnifying glasses to your toolkit if they are not already present. Display them in the classroom to build interest and start your kids talking about the possibilities. Remind students about the jobs ecologists perform in the field. Have them think about the interviews they conducted earlier in this unit. Activity 14 introduces your students to the specific area they will be studying as ecologists.

Soil is a mixture of rocks, minerals, and decaying plants and animals. It can be very different from one place to another, but usually consists of some organic and inorganic materials, water, and air. The amount of water can be linked with the climate and other characteristics of the region in which the soil is found. The composition of soil affects the plants and, in turn, it affects the animals that can live in an area.

Sand, silt, and clay are the basic types of soil; most soils are made up of a combination of the three. The texture of the soil, how it looks and feels, depends upon the amount of each type of soil in that particular sample. The type of soil varies from place to place on our planet and can even vary from one place to another in your own backyard.

Soil quality can be defined as the capacity of a specific kind of soil to provide nutrition to plants and drain water. The pH factor is used to measure a soil's acidity, helping growers to determine the best kinds of plants to cultivate in a given area. This can help save costs, because a gardener or farmer won't be purchasing plants that couldn't grow in his area. It also allows growers to determine the types and amounts of fertilizers to use to make the ground more suitable for growing. Activity 15 teaches students to measure and determine soil quality.

Although it is true that the plants in your local ecosystem rely on the soil for fertility, all organisms on Earth owe their lives to a simple element: carbon. Carbon is constantly passed along through the biosphere in various forms. It is found in all living things, in water, and in the land itself. It becomes carbon dioxide in the air, sugars in plants, and calcium carbonate in the land and the shells of animals. Moving from the air, to the bodies of living things, to water and back, carbon is cyclical. Activity 16 helps students understand the carbon cycle.

Like carbon, Earth's water moves through a cycle. From liquid, to vapor, and back to water, it is transferred from organism to atmosphere to land. The sun's heat provides energy to evaporate water from the Earth's surface. Plants also lose water to the air through transpiration. The water vapor eventually condenses, forming tiny droplets in clouds. When the clouds meet cool air over land, precipitation happens, and water returns to the Earth.

Because water is crucial to the existence of all living things, its quality is important to take note of. Water is exceptionally solvent—this means it can mix with many different substances. Sometimes this can be a problem, making water vulnerable to pollution or contamination. Contamination occurs from natural elements like soil, silt, or organic decay. When water is contaminated, it has a muddy, mucky look and gives off an unpleasant odor. If polluted, water may or may not give off an odor or look different. Pollution occurs when humans release sewage, chemicals, or industrial waste into water sources.

Contaminated or polluted water is still part of the water cycle and will evaporate, eventually returning to the Earth's surface as precipitation. This will further pollute the freshwater supply the precipitation falls into. By evaluating and understanding the quality of local water supplies, children will have an appreciation for the fragility of this nonrenewable resource, and hopefully take measures to protect it. Activity 17 allows your students to experiment with water quality and the water cycle.

Activity 12

MAPPING YOUR LOCAL ECOSYSTEM

Subjects and Skills	Science, social studies, geography
Rationale	It is important to help students put the subjects they study into perspective. By mapping their local ecosystem, students will be personally invested in the unit.
Objectives	Students will identify the various ecosystems present in the immediate area of their schoolyard.
Activity Preparation	1. Make or locate (check your city offices, fire department, or police department) a large map of your area, including open spaces and areas with buildings.
Activity Procedures	2. Use the large map to decide on an area that students can explore on foot. Use a pencil to outline this onto the map. (Teachers, you may want to make smaller copies of the area so students can each have their own map in their field journals.)
	3. Walk the area with field journals, making notes and/or taking photographs of different ecosystems.
	4. After returning to the classroom, use colored pencils to mark the locations of all of the ecosystems observed. Students should use different patterns or symbols to differentiate and create a key for areas like buildings, parking lots, streams, trees, paths, roads, gardens, playgrounds, ponds, fields, hedges, and walls.
	5. Add to the map any details the students observed. Depending on the season, students may have noticed a bird's nest or a beaver's dam. They may have noticed a stream bed eroding, an area full of litter, an oil spill, or a matted down clump of grass where a deer slept.
	6. Display the map in the classroom.
Materials Needed	local map field journals pencils colored pencils camera film
Vocabulary	**map**—a representation of a place

Activity 13

ECOSYSTEMS WITHIN ECOSYSTEMS

Subjects and Skills	Science, geography
Rationale	All living things interact with all other things—living and nonliving—in their environments.
Objectives	Students will observe the interactions of living things within their local ecosystem.
Activity Preparation	1. Remind students of the interdependence of the different occupants of an ecosystem. Use the mini-ecosystems as a springboard for this discussion. Go over the colored and labeled local map from the previous activity.
Activity Procedures	1. Take another walk, making additional observations and taking more photographs. 2. Pay special attention to living things interacting with other living and nonliving things. For example, a squirrel crossing a road is interacting with the road and possibly the drivers on that road, ivy climbing up a building is interacting with the walls of the building, and a line of ants marching along the floor of the woods is interacting with each other and the dirt, twigs, and grasses they are marching over. 3. When the walk is completed, have students write some of the interactions found on sticky notes and place them on the large map in the location they were found. Talk about the diversity of life and habitats surrounding your school. 4. Finally, have small groups of students choose an area from the map and create a poster charting the living and the nonliving things found in each area.
Materials Needed	field journals pencils camera film sticky notes poster paper or poster board markers
Vocabulary	**living**—alive **nonliving**—inanimate, not alive **diversity**—differing from one another

Activity 14

A Square Yard

Subjects and Skills	Science, mathematics
Rationale	By personalizing this unit with a specified observation and activity site, students will personally identify with the lessons and realize the impact each of them has on our environment. It will also give students a chance to apply your teaching about food chains, energy transfer, and ecological relationships.
Objectives	Students will identify the components that make up an ecosystem. Students will measure and mark off an observation site on their school grounds.
Activity Preparation	1. Choose a place to observe and use as an experiment site for the next few activities. This could be as large as several square yards or as small as one square yard. Make sure you have permission to dig, plant, and garden in this space.
Activity Procedures	1. Take students to the chosen site and have them measure and stake off the entire square. Have them pay close attention to their measurements—remember, they are scientists choosing a location in which to set up an outdoor lab. 2. Once the area is measured and staked, have them mark it off by tying twine or rope between the stakes. They could set up a sign sharing the purpose of the area and identifying it as an experiment site, requesting that visitors leave it undisturbed. 3. Once the area is prepped, have them find a quiet place to sit and observe, making their initial observations and illustrations about the site. This should be a time of free observation—there will be other times that their observations will be specific to plants, animals, and the like. Encourage them to draw or write about anything they choose to focus their observations on.
Materials Needed	wooden stakes rope or twine tape measure, trundle wheel, yardsticks, or other measuring device a signpost and prepared sign field journal colored pencils pencils sign reproducible on p. 67
Vocabulary	**observation site**—the site where observations and experiments will take place

This is an ecological experiment site being used by

Please do not disturb the area or any equipment.

© Prufrock Press • *Hands-On Ecology*

This page may be photocopied or reproduced with permission for student use.

Activity 15

SOIL QUALITY

Subjects and Skills	Science
Rationale	Researching the soil quality in the observation area will give students an understanding of pollution levels.
Objectives	Students will determine the composition and quality of the soil in their observation area.
Activity Preparation	1. Use a science or gardening catalog to order soil pH test strips or a soil quality test kit. 2. Discuss with the class the differences in soil quality—the different factors involved, the influence each of these factors holds, the different layers of soil, the different tests scientists use to determine soil quality, and the different ways people can improve soil quality.
Activity Procedures	1. Go to the test site and have students work in small groups to take soil samples. Students should try to dig at least 1 foot down to get an appropriate sample. 2. Using their sample, each small group should complete the Soil Quality Analysis handout. Students should record their findings on the Soil Quality Analysis Recording Sheet.
Materials Needed	shovels field journals pencils pH test strips Soil Quality Analysis handout Soil Quality Analysis Recording Sheet large glass or plastic beakers or jars water drop cloth or large sheets of paper
Vocabulary	**texture**—the feel of an object **humus**—the nutrient-rich, organic portion of soil **chemistry**—the make-up of matter **acidity**—the level of hydrogen concentration present in a compound **alkalinity**—the capacity of water to neutralize itself **pH**—a measure of acidity and alkalinity on a scale of seven

Soil Quality Analysis

When measuring soil quality, we need to evaluate the physical, chemical, and biological features present.

Physical Properties

Texture Activity 1

✿ Fill a jar one third full of your soil sample.

✿ Add water until the jar is two thirds full.

✿ Shake the jar for 1 minute and let it settle overnight.

✿ The next day, draw on your Soil Quality Analysis Recording Sheet what the soil in your jar looks like. The coarse sand should have settled first, followed by the silt, and then the clay.

Texture Activity 2

✿ Moisten some soil.

✿ Take a small amount in your hand and squeeze it as hard as you can.

✿ Open your hand and draw what it looks like.

✿ If the soil holds together, forming a cast, then it has a high percentage of clay.

✿ Record your observations on your recording sheet.

Humus Activity

✿ Take a 1-foot deep sample of soil.

✿ Look closely at its color.

✿ If your sample is dark, then it has humus and is fertile.

✿ Record your observations.

Chemical Properties

Simple pH Test

✿ Take a small sample of soil.

✿ Mix equal parts soil and water in a jar and shake.

✿ Dip your pH test strips into the solution and record your findings. (Your paper will change colors—you should compare it to the color chart that comes with the paper strips in order to identify the results.)

✿ Your paper will reflect the acidity or alkalinity of the soil you are testing.

Name: _____ Date _____

pH Reading	Meaning
< 5.6	Strongly Acidic
5.6 – 6.2	Moderately Acidic
6.2 – 6.7	Slightly Acidic
6.7 – 7.3	Neutral
7.3 – 7.9	Slightly Alkaline
7.9 – 8.5	Moderately Alkaline
> 8.5	Strongly Alkaline

✳ The pH scale measures soil acidity or alkalinity from 0 (extremely acidic) to 14 (extremely alkaline) with a reading of around 7 being neutral.

✳ Soil with a pH of from 6.0 to 7.0 (slightly acidic) is ideal for most plants.

✳ Soil testing can provide basic information about the nutrient content and plant-growing capacity. Gardeners and farmers can use this information to improve the soil quality before they plant.

✳ Write your findings on your recording sheet.

Biological Properties

Earthworm Check

❀ Dig up a 1' x 1' square of earth, trying to dig at least 6 inches down.

❀ Spread your soil on a drop cloth or large piece of paper.

❀ Record the measurements of the sample you dug out—width and depth.

❀ Sift through the soil, carefully removing and counting the earthworms and other creatures present.

❀ Record your findings on your Soil Quality Analysis Recording Sheet.

❀ Earthworms are important to the fertility of soil—so the more the merrier!

© Prufrock Press • *Hands-On Ecology*
This page may be photocopied or reproduced with permission for student use.

Soil Quality Analysis Recording Sheet

Physical Properties

Texture Activity 1

❀ In the box below, draw a picture of what the soil in your jar looks like after it sat overnight.

_____

Texture Activity 2

❀ Do you think your soil has a high percentage of clay? How can you tell?

_____

_____

_____

Texture Activity 3

❀ Do you think your soil has humus? _____

❀ Is it fertile? How can you tell?

_____

_____

_____

Name: _____ Date _____

Chemical Properties

Simple pH Test

✿ What color did your pH paper turn when you dipped it in the jar?

_____

✿ Compare your paper to the color chart. What does the chart give as your pH reading?

_____

✿ Is your soil sample alkaline? Acidic? Somewhere in between?

_____

Biological Properties

Earthworm Check

✿ What is the **width** of the sample you dug up? _____

✿ What is the **depth** of the sample you dug up? _____

✿ How many earthworms were in your sample?_____

✿ How many other creatures were in your sample? _____

© Prufrock Press • *Hands-On Ecology*
This page may be photocopied or reproduced with permission for student use.

Activity 16

UNDERSTANDING THE CARBON CYCLE

Subjects and Skills	Science
Rationale	It is important to understand that carbon is essential to all life on Earth.
Objectives	Students will understand the movements in the cycle of carbon on our planet.
Activity Preparation	1. Make an overhead of The Carbon Cycle handout on p. 74. 2. Engage students in a discussion about the carbon cycle and the impact humans are having upon it. 3. This activity can be done in two ways: as an interactive discussion with students filling out the carbon cycle chart for their journals as you discuss each piece or as a quiz after your discussion with students filling out a blank chart.
Activity Procedures	1. Use the transparency of the carbon cycle to walk students through it, explaining the importance of carbon to every living thing. Fill in the chart as you go along.
Materials Needed	The Carbon Cycle handout pencils transparency overhead overhead markers
Vocabulary	**carbon cycle**—the cycle of the Earth's carbon from an inorganic state to an organic one

The Carbon Cycle

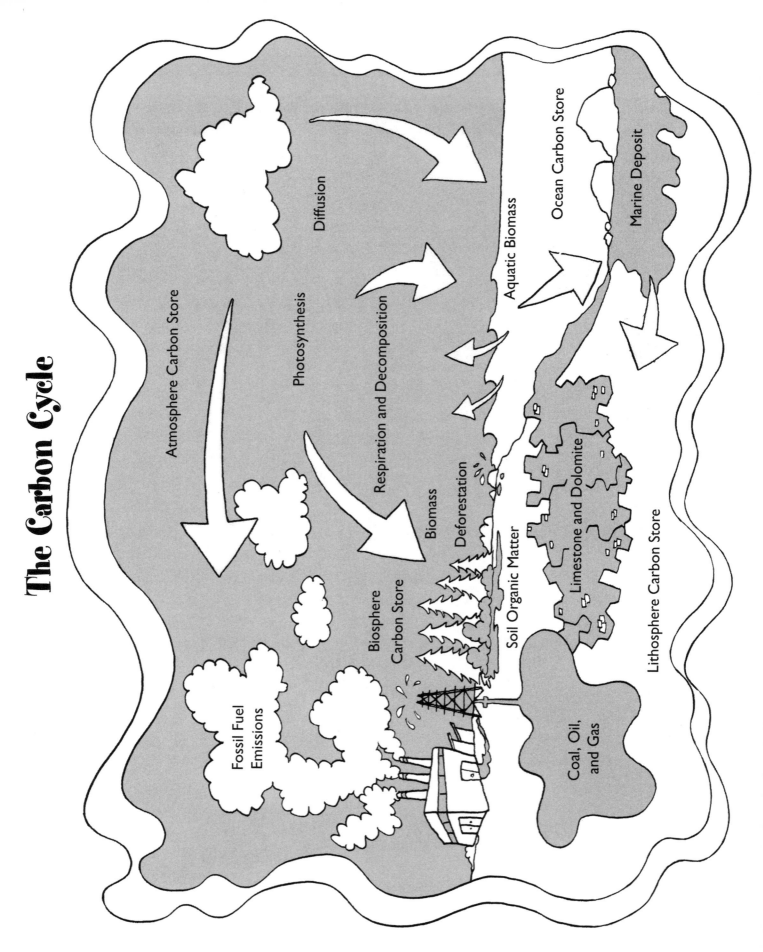

© Prufrock Press • *Hands-On Ecology*
This page may be photocopied or reproduced with permission for student use.

Activity 17

WATER QUALITY

Subjects and Skills	Science
Rationale	Water is vital to all living things and plays a crucial role in supporting life on Earth. Because of its solvency, it is extremely vulnerable to pollution. Therefore, students need to understand the delicate balance of fresh water and the dependency we have on it, so that they can identify steps to take to protect the Earth's water supply against pollution.
Objectives	Students will understand the movements of the water cycle and the impact water pollution has on the environment.
Activity Preparation	1. Discuss the importance of the water cycle and the potential impact of water pollution on life within an ecosystem. 2. Share the water cycle diagram, discussing the process by which water is recycled in the biosphere. 3. Collect several different water samples (e.g., spring water, distilled water, pond water, creek water, tap water, aquarium water).
Activity Procedures	1. Have students work in small groups; either focusing on one sample and sharing their results with the class, or rotating around and testing each sample. 2. Ask them to follow the directions on the experiment handout. If each group is testing each sample, they should have a separate experiment handout for each sample.
Materials Needed	different water samples beakers or other small containers for each sample pH paper microscope plastic or glass slides The Water Cycle handout Water Quality Experiment handout
Vocabulary	**water cycle**—the cycle water goes through within the environment **solvency**—the ability to dissolve **pollution**—environmental contamination

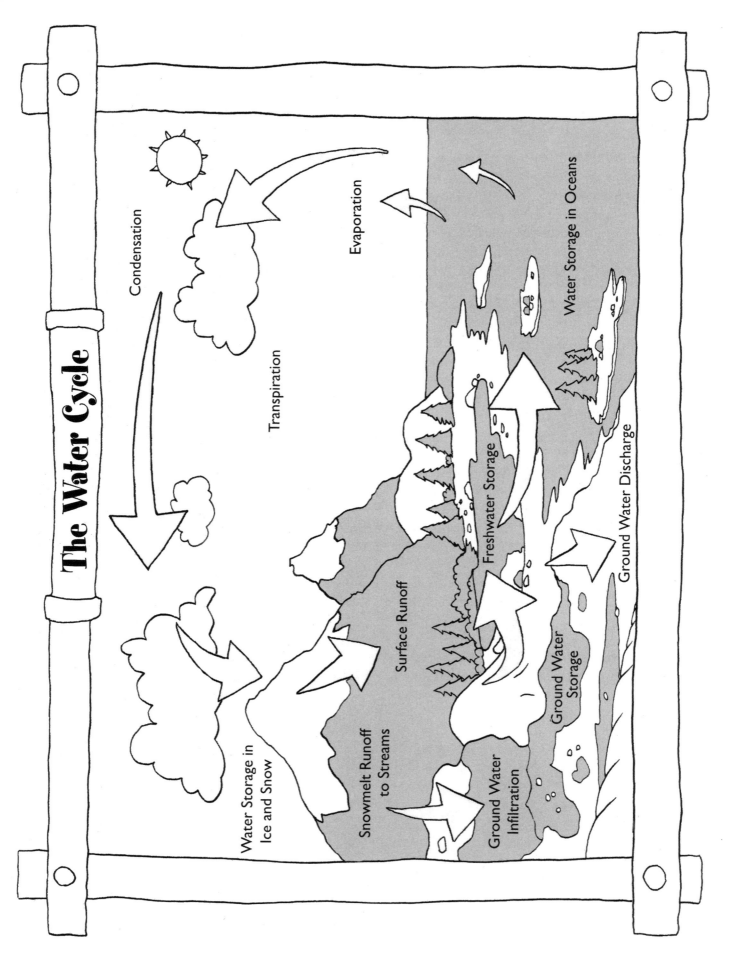

The Water Cycle

Condensation

Evaporation

Transpiration

Water Storage in Oceans

Freshwater Storage

Ground Water Discharge

Water Storage in Ice and Snow

Surface Runoff

Snowmelt Runoff to Streams

Ground Water Storage

Ground Water Infiltration

© Prufrock Press • *Hands-On Ecology*
This page may be photocopied or reproduced with permission for student use.

Water Quality Experiment

Procedures to follow with your sample:

1. Smell your sample to see if there is a detectable odor. Record your observations on the data chart.
2. Describe the clarity of the water on your data chart.
3. Dip the pH paper into your sample to test the acidity of the water. Record your data.
4. Finally, look at a sample of your water under the microscope. Look for bacteria or other small organisms swimming in it.
5. Record your observations.

Water Quality Data			
Test	Odor		
	Clarity		
	pH		
	Bacteria		
Results			
Conclusions			

On lined paper, write a paragraph that explains why, based on your data, drinking water should be tested regularly.

© Prufrock Press • *Hands-On Ecology*
This page may be photocopied or reproduced with permission for student use.

Chapter

Studying Populations

Although it may seem like there is an even distribution of life across the globe, it is actually very discrepant. In some deserts and in the coldest parts of Antarctica, no organisms can tolerate the tough conditions. On a smaller scale, one side of a creek may be teeming with life, whereas the other has few occupants. One tree can be the home to mosses, lichens, and insects, while another tree nearby houses none.

When scientists study populations, they are interested in what kinds of organisms are present where and what biological factors contribute to the presence or absence of certain species. They also look through the history of the area to discover any patterns that may need to be considered, especially in the case of endangered species.

Because it is very difficult to count all of the individual organisms living in an ecosystem, ecologists rely on a method called *sampling*. A square metal, wooden, or wire frame is placed on the floor of the ecosystem that is being studied. Scientists count all of the organisms present within the frame, or *quadrant*, and record their data. This is repeated regularly so patterns are more likely to be noticed. Activities 18 and 19 take students through the process of studying ecosystems using sampling.

It is important for ecologists to not only understand what animals can be found in a particular ecosystem, but what their role in that system is. Organisms have a specific function within their habitat; this is known as their *ecological niche*. If several animals performed the same role (e.g., eating a specific insect to keep that population under control), then they would be competing and one could possibly drive the other to extinction.

Similar animals are sometimes able to occupy the same space, provided their roles are different. For example, the Crossbill Finch, Bullfinch, and Greenfinch are able to live near one another because they have different niches. They have adapted different dietary needs and methods of obtaining the food that they eat. The Crossbill eats the seeds from pine cones using its unique criss-crossing bill to reach in between the slots. The Greenfinch uses its strong, sharp, pointed bill to crunch on hard seeds and nuts. Finally, the Bullfinch has an extremely strong, but short, bill that can easily snip juicy buds off a fruit tree.

Evolving to be able to consume and obtain certain kinds of food is only one type of adaptation organisms have for surviving in their habitats. Animals and plants have different methods of protecting themselves. Some animals, like chameleons, are able to change color to blend in more easily to their surroundings. Others, like lightning bugs, have a terrible taste and a method for signaling to predators that they don't taste very good. Plants, like some desert cactuses, have prickly spines to help hold water and to keep herbivores away from them.

Slugs and snails don't have feet, but they are able to move from place to place because they have evolved a method of locomotion—they have powerful muscles on the bottom of their bodies that ripple, pushing them along a slime trail. Some birds, like the hawk, can use their large wings to coast on the wind and glide along, using less energy as they concentrate on the ground below to search for food.

Every organism has specific adaptations that make it possible for it to obtain food, move around, and protect itself. By becoming good observers, kids will learn to pick up on the unique methods organisms use to survive. Activity 20 teaches students more about adaptation and survival.

Activity 18

ANIMAL POPULATIONS

Subjects and Skills	Science
Rationale	Ecologists study the distribution of organisms to discover the biological and physical factors that influence particular species. They compare this information to historical patterns to see how population distribution could change in the future. This helps to identify and save potentially endangered species. Students can learn about specific organisms in their areas and see what they can do to ensure their survival.
Objectives	Students will identify animals and tracks present in their observation site.
Activity Preparation	1. Collect various wildlife field guides for your local area. 2. Review procedures and expectations for working in the field.
Activity Procedures	1. Plan for an extended period of observation time in the staked off area. 2. Have students choose a location in which to sit quietly, observing the animals that come into view. Students should use their checklist of animal types to tally the different animal life they see. Remind them that they are looking for all species: mammals, reptiles, amphibians, and insects. 3. They should make detailed observations and drawings of the different species on their observation record to be placed in their field journal. 4. Finally, students should place their hula hoops or frames on the ground, and using magnifying glasses, they should get on their hands and knees to observe the grasses and the dirt closely to see the smaller populations present in their ecosystem. 5. Engage students in a discussion when you go back to the classroom about the different species they each observed in their study area. Did they all see the same animals? Why or why not? What type was the most prevalent? Why do they think there was more of this type of animal than any other?
Materials Needed	field journals hula hoops or 2' x 2' square frames Animal Observation Chart and Tally Sheet pens pencils colored pencils magnifying glasses

Vocabulary   **mammal**—warm blooded animals with hair or fur and a backbone, whose mothers secrete milk for their young

amphibian—cold-blooded animals that begin life in the water and usually transform to land-dwelling adults

reptile—cold-blooded vertebrate that lays eggs and has scales

insect—an invertebrate with three body segments, three pairs of legs, two sets of wings (usually), a pair of antennae, and compound eyes

Name: _____ Date _____

Animal Observation Chart and Tally Sheet

	Tally	Observations
Insects		
Reptiles		
Amphibians		
Mammals		

Activity 19

PLANT POPULATIONS

Subjects and Skills	Science
Rationale	Ecologists study the distribution of organisms to discover the biological and physical factors that influence particular species. They compare this information to historical patterns to see how population distribution could change in the future. This helps to identify and save potential endangered species.
	Students can learn about specific organisms in their areas and see what they can do to ensure their survival.
Objectives	Students will identify different plant species present in their observation site.
Activity Preparation	1. Collect different plant and wildflower field guides.
	2. Review procedures and expectations for working in the field.
Activity Procedures	1. This activity will be performed in the same way as the previous activity, except that students will focus on identifying the different plant populations within their staked off area.
Materials Needed	Plant Life Observation Chart and Tally Sheet
	hula hoops or 2' x 2' square frames
	field guides
	field journals
	pens
	pencils
	colored pencils
	magnifying glasses
Vocabulary	**herb**—an upright, nonwoody plant
	tree—a plant with a main trunk that supports a leafy crown
	shrubs—plants with many woody stems reaching close to the ground
	vines—plants with long, twisting stems

Plant Life Observation Chart and Tally Sheet

Inside the box, please tally the number of plants you see within your framed area

[ ]

On the lines below, write the names of any plant species you can identify.

_____

_____

_____

_____

_____

_____

_____

_____

_____

_____

Activity 20

ADAPTATIONS

Subjects and Skills	Science
Rationale	All organisms are adapted specifically to survive in the environment in which they live.
Objectives	Students will identify the adaptations animals have developed for survival in their environment.

Activity Preparation

1. Lead a class discussion on the various ways animals have adapted for survival in their environments and the ways they have evolved based on the environment in which they live.
2. Share various examples to give students an understanding of what they will look for when they observe the organisms in their observation site and in the mini-ecosystems within the classroom.
3. List, for your own records, the various adaptations each organism within the ecosystems displays.

Activity Procedures

1. Have students choose the name of one of the classroom ecosystems out of a box or basket.
2. They will work in small groups taking note of the structural adaptations each organism in the ecosystem—plants and animals—have for survival.
3. Discuss the findings from the classroom ecosystems to find out if the students understand what they are looking for before heading outside to the observation site.
4. Have the students take their rings or hula hoops out into the staked-off site. In pairs or small groups, have them cast their hoops—away from other groups—to mark a personal observation site.
5. Have them use their journals or the handout and field guides to list each organism found within their hoops, then identify each organism's adaptations.

Materials Needed

hula hoops or large plastic rings
field journals
Classroom Ecosystems Adaptations handout
Observation Site Organism Adaptations handout
pencils

Vocabulary   **adaptation**—a behavioral or structural modification an organism has evolved in
                order to survive in its environment
              survival—remaining alive
              camouflage—a way of hiding by blending in with one's environment
              locomotion—the ability to move

Classroom Ecosystems Adaptations

Organism	
Adaptations to Obtain Food	
Adaptation to Move From Place to Place	
Adaptations to Protect Itself	

© Prufrock Press • *Hands-On Ecology*
This page may be photocopied or reproduced with permission for student use.

Observation Site Organism Adaptations

Organism	
Adaptations to Obtain Food	
Adaptation to Move From Place to Place	
Adaptations to Protect itself	

© Prufrock Press • *Hands-On Ecology*
This page may be photocopied or reproduced with permission for student use.

Chapter

Human Impact on the Environment

Soil erosion is natural. It becomes a problem when human activities cause it to occur at a faster rate than it is supposed to. Wind and water are the main causes of soil erosion. Two factors contribute to the amount of soil that is carried away during the process: speed and plant cover. Speed refers to how fast the water or the wind is moving because the faster it moves, the more soil it can take away. Plant cover is important to consider because plants can protect the soil under them, holding it in place. Bare soil erodes more easily.

The loss of protective vegetation through deforestation, overgrazing, plowing, and fire makes soil vulnerable to erosion because plants slow runoff (water flowing over land) so more water is able to soak into the ground. In addition, plants' roots hold soil in place so it is harder to wash away, and their leaves soften the impact of raindrops before they hit the ground, which lessens their ability to erode. Activity 21 explores erosion and its effects on soil.

Although it is one of our most important resources, the air in our atmosphere is often polluted to a point where it is dangerous to breathe. Air pollution can be seen in its effects: smog, acid rain, the greenhouse effect, and ozone depletion. Each of these holds serious implications for our health and the well-being of our natural environment.

Some air pollution is the result of particles being released into the air from the burning of fossil fuels, improper waste management, and the exhaust from motor vehicles. Noxious gases like sulfur dioxide, carbon monoxide, and other chemical vapors can cause additional chemical reactions in the atmosphere, resulting in acid rain. When a chemical like carbon monoxide interacts with the water droplets in the air, the water becomes acidified and can cause serious damage to the environment, as well as man-made things like buildings and bridges. The acid can react with the chemicals in certain metals, wearing them down and causing millions of dollars worth of damage. The acidified rainwater can run into streams, oceans, and lakes, killing thousands of organisms and throwing off the balance of an ecosystem. Some damaged ecosystems are unable to recover and thousands of populations can become threatened and endangered.

The greenhouse effect is believed to come from the buildup of carbon dioxide gas in the atmosphere. Carbon dioxide is released when certain fuels are burned. Although we learned that plants convert carbon dioxide back to oxygen, the overproduction of carbon dioxide from human activities is higher than the world's plants can process. The situation is made worse because many of the earth's forests are being removed and plant life is being damaged by acid rain. The amount of carbon dioxide in the air is continuing to increase and trap heat close to the surface of our earth. This changes the temperature, which affects the overall climate—even a few degrees difference can affect us all. Scientists worry that a rising global temperature may cause the polar ice caps to melt, forcing a rise in sea levels, resulting in planetary flooding. Activities 22, 23, 24, and 25 take a look at the effects of several types of pollution on our ecosystem.

Activity 21

EROSION

Subjects and Skills	Science
Rationale	By understanding how erosion happens, children can apply their knowledge to help reverse some of its effects by planting trees and shrubs.
Objectives	Students will recognize signs of erosion within their observation site.
Activity Preparation	1. Take the potted plant out of its pot, keeping the soil intact, and discuss how the plant's roots help to hold its soil in place. Ask the students for ideas and hypotheses about what would happen if the plant was not in a pot, but in the ground with water running over it. 2. Holding it over a bucket or pan, use a watering can or hose spigot to pour a constant stream of water over the soil and roots of the plant. Have students share their observations. 3. Discuss the meaning of erosion and how water, wind, ice, snow, and other elements in nature contribute to erosion.
Activity Procedures	1. Take a walk to the observation site and have students make observations of the different signs of erosion they can see. 2. Have them draw and describe these signs within their field journal. 3. Back in the classroom, talk about the different signs of erosion the students found in the observation site and ways people could control erosion around drains, streams, and the edges of the sidewalk. 4. Talk about the placement of trees and shrubs. Could planting these in places likely to have erosion take place help prevent it?
Materials Needed	potted plant bucket watering can or hose field journals
Vocabulary	**erosion**—wearing away, disintegrating, or disappearing by wind, water, or other natural elements **weathering**—to endure the action of atmospheric events

Activity 22

AIR QUALITY

Subjects and Skills	Science, mathematics, language arts
Rationale	There are different particles moving throughout the air, and students can discover whether the air around their school contains mostly natural particles or pollutants.
Objectives	Students will formulate and test a hypothesis, analyzing the results.
Activity Preparation	1. Lead a discussion with students, helping them to come up different ideas about where to place their collection cards. 2. Remind them that particles in the air will vary from place to place.
Activity Procedures	1. Have students cut a 3 cm x 3 cm square in the center of three index cards. Have them write their name on the front of the cards. 2. They should then put a strip of clear packaging tape on the other side of the card, covering the hole and leaving the sticky side exposed on the side with their name. 3. Have them attach the cards to trees, poles, walls, or other solid objects in the various locations students have chosen to test with the sticky side facing outward (exposed to the air). 4. When they come back into the classroom, have them fill out the prediction section of their data sheet. 5. After 24 hours, return to take the cards down. Bring them back into the classroom for analysis. 6. Ask the students to place their 1-centimeter square grid paper on the back of their index cards and count the number of particles within one square. They could use magnifying glasses or microscopes if they wish. Students should use that number to calculate the number of particles there are on the entire square. 7. Have students record the number of particles on their data sheet and write the specific particles they are able to identify.
Materials Needed	Air Quality Data Sheet magnifying glass microscope index cards packaging tape 1 cm square grid paper

Vocabulary **atmosphere**—the mass of air surrounding the Earth
pollutants—substances that destroy the purity of air, water, or land
particles—very small pieces of solid or liquids

Name: _____ Date _____

Air Quality Data Sheet

Complete on Day 1:

1. Where did you place your data collection cards?

_____

_____

_____

2. How many particles per square centimeter do you think there will be in that area during a 24-hour period?

_____

3. Which site do you think will contain the most particle matter after a 24-hour period?

_____

4. Why do you think that?

_____

_____

_____

Complete on Day 2:

1. Which site had the most particle matter?

_____

2. How did this compare to your prediction?

_____

_____

© Prufrock Press • *Hands-On Ecology*
This page may be photocopied or reproduced with permission for student use.

3. Based on the data collected by the others in the class, what is the most highly polluted area on your school grounds?

_____

4. Why do you think this is?

_____

_____

_____

5. Why do you think different locations have different pollution levels?

_____

_____

_____

6. Are there any particles you can identify using the microscope or your magnifying glass?

_____

_____

_____

7. What are some of the categories you can divide the different types of particles into?

_____

_____

_____

Name: _____ Date _____

8. Do you think the temperature outside has any impact on the number of particles collected? If yes, what effect does it have?

_____

_____

_____

9. Do you think the weather has any impact? If yes, what effect does it have?

_____

_____

_____

10. Based on the results of your experiment, what recommendations could you make for reducing particle matter and improving air quality around your school?

_____

_____

_____

11. Now that you have completed this activity, why do you think it is important for scientists to continue to monitor air quality?

_____

_____

_____

© Prufrock Press • *Hands-On Ecology*
This page may be photocopied or reproduced with permission for student use.

Activity 23

ACID RAIN

Subjects and Skills	Science
Rationale	When acids come into contact with metals and other objects, the effects can be significant. Corrosion occurs and man-made structures can deteriorate, while pollution levels rise in our environments.
Objectives	Students will see the effects acid has on metals and understand the environmental issues that can arise when we face increased levels of acid in our rain.
Activity Preparation	1. Discuss the term *acid rain* and help students to understand what problems it can cause.
Activity Procedures	1. Divide students into several small groups—one for each of the metal types.
	2. Have each group set up two jars—one with a sample of their metal covered with white vinegar and one with a sample of their metal covered with distilled water.
	3. Dip a strip of pH paper in the vinegar for several seconds and record the result.
	4. Dip a second strip of pH paper in the water for several seconds and record that result, as well.
	5. Seal the top of each jar tightly and place in a warm, dry place for 2 weeks.
	6. At the end of the 2 weeks, have the students remove the metal samples, rinse them off, and record their observations.
	7. Have students record their answers to the questions on the bottom of the observation recording sheet.
	8. Lead a discussion about the students' findings.
Materials Needed	small samples of several different metals (e.g., copper pennies [minted prior to 1983], steel nails, aluminum foil, brass pieces, lead pieces, or zinc) distilled water white vinegar pH paper and chart glass jars with sealable lids The Effect of Acid on Metals handout
Vocabulary	**acid rain**—cloud or rain droplets containing pollutants **corrosion**—the destruction of metal by a chemical reaction

The Effect of Acid on Metals

1. Draw what your metals looked like before the experiment in the box below. Describe it on the lines below the box.

```



```

_____

_____

_____

_____

_____

_____

2. What is the pH of the vinegar water? _____

3. What is the pH of the distilled water? _____

© Prufrock Press • *Hands-On Ecology*
This page may be photocopied or reproduced with permission for student use.

Name: _____ Date _____

4. After your metals have been in their jars for 2 weeks, draw a picture of each in the boxes below. Label each. Describe any changes that have taken place.

5. What surprised you about the appearance of your metals?

_____

_____

6. Compare your results to those of other students. Which metals showed the most signs of corrosion?

_____

_____

7. Why do you think that is the case?

_____

_____

Activity 24

LOCAL WATER POLLUTION

Subjects and Skills	Science, mathematics
Rationale	Rainfall carries pollution from the air and can possibly contaminate local watersheds.
Objectives	Students will collect and test a sample of local rainwater to find out the levels of pollution that are going into our air.

Activity Preparation	1. This activity needs to be completed following a storm or rain shower, as rainwater is the ingredient you will be testing.
	
	 2. Refer back to earlier activity about water quality while discussing the various ways humans have impacted the Earth's fresh water supply. Brainstorm a list of different things people could change to preserve this dwindling supply.
	
	 3. Set up a collection drum prior to a forecasted rainy day. You could do this in two different ways:
	     a. Have students help create rain gauges out of 2-liter bottles by cutting off the tops and drawing measurements along the outside. Secure these in the ground in your observation site by digging small holes and partially burying the bottles.
	     b. Place a large bucket in your observation site and secure it using rope and stakes.

Activity Procedures	1. Copy the handout from the water quality activity. Students will use the same procedures and materials to test this water as they did to test the water samples in the previous activity.
Materials Needed	desired water collection containers different water samples beakers or other small containers for each sample pH paper microscope plastic or glass slides Water Quality Experiment handout from p. 75
Vocabulary	**contaminate**—to make unclean or impure **watershed**—the specific land area that drains water into a body of water **rain gauge**—a device for measuring rainfall

Activity 25

GLOBAL CLIMATE

Subjects and Skills	Science, mathematics
Rationale	There has been an increasing rise in global temperatures over the last few years, and students should understand the repercussions of a world where greenhouse gases are not held in check.
Objectives	Students will understand what the greenhouse effect is and its impact on our environment.
Activity Preparation	1. Discussion of the greenhouse effect:
	❀ The greenhouse effect is a natural phenomenon that allows the Earth to support life.
	❀ Without it, the Earth would be *very* cold.
	❀ Greenhouse gases act like a shield around the Earth, and radiation from the sun travels through the shield to the Earth's surface, bouncing back up as heat.
	❀ The heat cannot escape back through the shield, so the Earth warms up.
	❀ The problem is that there is an increase in greenhouse gases due to human pollution, so the Earth traps too much heat, causing global warming.
	2. Introduce the activity—a visual as to how the greenhouse effect actually works.
Activity Procedures	1. Divide the class into pairs—lab partners.
	2. Stand up each thermometer, using a ball of modeling clay. Fix one to the lid of the jar and one to the counter next to it. This activity should be completed in a sunny spot.
	3. Place the jar over the lid and tightly screw it on.
	4. Record the starting temperature on each thermometer.
	5. Continue recording temperatures every minute without touching any of the equipment.
	6. Continue for 10 minutes, then record observations and conclusions.
	7. Discuss that the air over the exposed thermometer is constantly changing and as the sun warms it, it is replaced by cooler air. Because the air in the jar cannot recirculate, it stays in the sunlight and gets warmer and warmer. Both the atmosphere and the jar allow light to enter, but trap that energy as it gets converted to heat.
	8. Have students set up line graphs to display their data.

Materials Needed   field journals
                    Mini-Greenhouse Effect Observation Sheet
                    graph paper
                    two thermometers per pair or small group of students
                    one large Mason jar or other glass jar with a screw-on lid per pair of students
                    modeling clay

Vocabulary   **ozone layer**—a layer of the atmosphere located about 20–30 miles above the Earth

greenhouse gases—gases that trap the heat of the sun in the Earth's atmosphere, producing the greenhouse effect

greenhouse effect—the warming of the lower part of the atmosphere and the surface of the Earth caused by converting solar radiation to heat

global warming—the warming of the Earth's atmosphere through the burning of fossil fuels

Mini-Greenhouse Effect Observation Sheet

Complete this activity, noting how the heat in the sealed jar differs from the heat freely circulating around the exposed thermometer.

	Time	Thermometer in Jar	Thermometer on Counter
1 minute			
2 minutes			
3 minutes			
4 minutes			
5 minutes			
6 minutes			
7 minutes			
8 minutes			
9 minutes			
10 minutes			

© Prufrock Press • *Hands-On Ecology*
This page may be photocopied or reproduced with permission for student use.

1. On graph paper, graph your results and compare the different temperatures.

2. What did you notice about the temperature of the air in the jar compared to the temperature of the air outside the jar?

_____

_____

_____

Because the air in the jar cannot circulate freely like the air outside the jar, the air continues to get warmer and warmer. Heat from the sun can enter the jar and warm the air by getting converted to heat energy, but the converted energy cannot escape back through the walls of the jar. This is similar to the way heat is trapped in the Earth's atmosphere. Sunlight passes through the atmosphere and warms the surface of the planet, but rather than being able to freely circulate, the energy gets trapped in by greenhouse gasses.

This greenhouse effect plays an important role in regulating the temperature of our planet. Without it, Earth would become a cold, barren place unable to support life. The problem is that because the burning of fossil fuels has increased as the human population's desire for energy has increased, too much heat is being released into the air, so the planet is getting too hot. This could have serious implications on the future well-being of our planet.

Chapter 6

Making a Contribution to Conservation

On April 22, 1970, Senator Gaylord Nelson founded the first Earth Day celebration. He wanted to use it as a vehicle for raising political awareness of the environment. Little did he know how the idea would catch on. At a time when rivers like the Cuyahoga River in Cleveland, OH, were catching fire from pollutants igniting, and smog hung over valleys, people were excited about this grassroots forum for expressing their concerns. More than 20 million demonstrators and thousands of schools participated in the first observance of Earth Day, and it is still being celebrated today.

That same year, President Richard Nixon created the Environmental Protection Agency (EPA) as a means of protecting the environment, as well as public health. Also in the 1970s, the Clean Air Act was amended, lead-based paints and the use of DDT were banned, Congress passed the Clean Water Act, and chlorofluorocarbons (CFCs) were banned, as they cause ozone depletion. Since the 1970s, and Senator Nelson's unique ploy to gain government awareness of the environmental crisis, numerous acts and regulations have been passed with agencies like the EPA continuing to work on finding new ways of making this planet even healthier. Activity 26 will introduce your students to these ecological events while they conduct an "Earth Day Internet Scavenger Hunt."

Children are the future of this planet. They will be the ones to find solutions to the environmental problems we are now facing. We need to do all that we can to nurture the love of nature that comes intrinsically bred in so many kids. Living things are fascinating. Capitalize on this love and interest and help your students form an ethic of conservationism and a love of all things living.

This section has numerous activities (Activities 27–34) to help you foster this caring attitude in your students. Use as many or as few of them as you want, alone or in conjunction with your Earth Day celebrations. Each is an activity that would fit in well with a schoolwide celebration of Earth Day, spearheaded and organized by your young ecologists. By using the knowledge and celebration of Earth Day as a springboard, you can ignite a passionate ecological awareness in those entrusted to you for their education.

Activity 26

EARTH DAY INTERNET SCAVENGER HUNT

Subjects and Skills	Science, language arts, technology
Rationale	Understanding the impact one person with one idea can make is the greatest lesson in the founding of Earth Day. Students can internalize this lesson and seek to make a difference themselves.
Objectives	Students will utilize technology to discover the history of Earth Day and several ways they can make an environmental impact, planning some of their own celebrations.
Activity Preparation	1. Make sure you have Internet access and check out the links to make sure they are not under construction. If you do not have Internet access in your school or classroom, print out the information from the Web sites listed and have students work in groups to find the information. If you find that some of the Web sites no longer work, you may want to create your own scavenger hunt on ecological issues using Web sites, books, magazines, or other resources. *Note:* When computers are limited, use this activity as a center that kids can work on with partners while you work with small groups on other activities, rotating everyone through all of the activities over the course of a school day. Pull everyone together after all of the students have completed the hunt to discuss their ideas for celebrating Earth Day this year.
Activity Procedures	1. Have students work alone or in pairs to find out the information on the Web sites listed on the scavenger hunt. 2. Discuss celebration ideas as a class, consolidating the class's ideas on the board or chart paper.
Materials Needed	chart paper markers Earth Day Internet Scavenger Hunt handout computers with Internet access
Vocabulary	**Earth Day**—a national day of observation to honor the protection of the environment

Earth Day Internet Scavenger Hunt

Follow the directions and go to each Web address listed to answer the questions on this page. When you are finished, you will be an expert on the subject of Earth Day and may even have some ideas for hosting your own celebration!

Go to http://epa.gov/history/topics/earthday/02.htm to find out about the history behind the first Earth Day.

Stay at that site for awhile. Find out the answers to the questions below:

1. Who was the founder of Earth Day?

_____

2. What was his primary goal for creating this day of ecological awareness?

_____

_____

_____

_____

3. Which federal act has given the means to "assess and abate" threats to the Great Lakes ecosystems?

_____

4. What, according to the founder, is the "fundamental issue" faced?

_____

_____

_____

_____

Name: _____ Date _____

Now, check out the site http://epa.gov/history/topics/earthday/08.htm to learn about some of the impacts the first Earth Day has had on our legislature.

1. List four things that the Environmental Protection Agency (EPA) has done since its founding following the first Earth Day.

_____

_____

_____

_____

2. In the third paragraph, the author says, "we must act as responsible stewards of our air, our water, and our land." What do you think she means by that?

_____

_____

_____

_____

3. Why does the author insist that every American must help to ensure "environmental protections?" Do you agree? Why or why not?

_____

_____

_____

_____

Name: _____ Date _____

Read through some of the suggestions and links at the following Web sites:

- ❀ http://www.epa.gov/earthday/home.htm
- ❀ http://www.epa.gov/earthday/community.htm
- ❀ http://www.epa.gov/earthday/classroom.htm
- ❀ http://www.epa.gov/earthday/shopping.htm

Make a plan. What can you do to help celebrate Earth Day on April 22 and every day? Think about it and write some of your ideas on the brainstorming web. Use these as a springboard in your class discussions as you come up with a way to celebrate as a class this year.

© Prufrock Press • *Hands-On Ecology*
This page may be photocopied or reproduced with permission for student use.

Name: _____ Date _____

Brainstorming Web

Use this brainstorming web to organize your thinking and plan your Earth Day celebrations.

Celebrating
Earth Day

What can you do to celebrate on April 22?	What can you do to celebrate everyday?

What preparations will you need to make?	What preparations will you need to make?

© Prufrock Press • Hands-On Ecology
This page may be photocopied or reproduced with permission for student use.

Activity 27

HOSTING A SPEAKER OR AN ASSEMBLY

Subjects and Skills   Science, language arts, social studies

Rationale   By hosting a speaker or setting up an awareness assembly, children can have an active role in spreading environmental awareness.

Objectives   Students will plan an assembly or host a speaker to spread environmental awareness within their school.

Activity Preparation
1. Use local contacts (e.g., parents, board members, city hall) to find community members who would be willing to donate their time to speak to your class or school about the ways kids can contribute to ecological conservation. Sometimes local energy companies have outreach or education programs.
2. Talk with your principal about the steps you need to take to organize a classroom or schoolwide speaker.

Activity Procedures
1. As a class, brainstorm ideas of who you could invite in to speak. If appropriate, decide whether your class would like to host a schoolwide speaker or just have someone talk to them.
2. If they decide to invite the speaker in to talk just to the class, invite them to think about what kinds of questions they could ask, what sort of reception would be nice for the speaker, and what they could do in advance to make his or her visit more successful.
3. If they decide, and the principal approves, to host an energy awareness assembly for the entire school, they will need to do a little more planning. Encourage your students to think about the following considerations:
   ✿ Who will contact the speaker and invite him or her to speak to the school?
   ✿ What will the focus of the assembly be?
   ✿ How long will it last?
   ✿ What kinds of preparations are required by the school building and grounds department?
   ✿ Will students act as greeters and hosts for his or her visit?
   ✿ How will the location of the assembly be decorated?
   ✿ Will other community members be invited?
   ✿ Will the local newspapers be notified?
   ✿ What other considerations may come up?

4. Begin planning specifics, including individual jobs each child will be asked to perform as the class hosting the event. Detailed planning will make an event like this seem seamless and give students an understanding of what goes into large event hosting.

Materials Needed contacts for local speakers or community members willing to talk to kids about energy conservation or environmental awareness

Vocabulary **environmental awareness**—consideration of the impact a person has on the natural environment

Activity 28

WRITING AND PERFORMING

Subjects and Skills	Science, language arts, dramatic arts
Rationale	Giving students a chance to experience a topic using a variety of modalities such as acting gives them greater understanding and ownership of the topics they study.
Objectives	Students will read a variety of short texts encouraging environmental conservation and rewrite them as readers' theater scripts, which will then be performed.

Activity Preparation

1. Collect numerous stories and picture books with environmental themes. (See the appendix for a limited list of titles.)

Activity Procedures

1. Have students work in pairs or small groups.
2. Give them time to read several of the books and stories you have collected before choosing one that interests the group.
3. Ask them to use that book as a guide to writing a reader's theater script. *Note:* Reader's theater scripts are written devoid of action. They are simply dialogue that the readers read, using the various inflections to convey emotion. If action is important to the plot and can't be left out completely, a narrator can be used to read about what is going on.
4. Give them class time over several days or weeks to read, write, and rehearse.
5. Finally, have a performance day. This could be done in several different ways:
   ✿ Groups can perform for each other within the classroom.
   ✿ Parents and other family members can be invited in to see the performances in the classroom.
   ✿ Performances can be part of an Earth Day assembly.
   ✿ Students can perform for younger classes.
   ✿ Be creative—your students worked hard and, after all, each performance will have an underlying message of ecological action.

Materials Needed   books
paper
pencils

Vocabulary   **conservation**—the wise use of natural resources

Activity 29

TREE PLANTING EVENT

Subjects and Skills	Science, language arts, social studies
Rationale	Children will understand that everyone can make a difference and have a positive impact on the environment.
Objectives	Students will organize and hold a tree planting event.
Activity Preparation	1. Contact local nurseries or landscaping companies to see if any would like to donate a ball and burlap tree for you to plant during your event. This may be easier than you think if you will be having local news coverage and agree to mention where the tree was donated from.
Activity Procedures	1. Decide where the tree planting event will take place. Will you plant the tree on school grounds or a local senior center or animal shelter?
	2. Secure written permission from the owner of the land where you will be planting.
	3. Contact local newspapers and television and radio stations to advertise the event.
	4. The tree could be planted to commemorate an influential member of society, the school, an accomplishment, or Earth Day. Whatever it is planted for, make sure it is a celebration. Have kids speak to the gathered audience about the importance of trees, conservation, and environmental awareness. Have the principal say a few words. Invite the superintendent or mayor to throw the first shovelful of dirt on the tree as students and teachers lower it into the hole. Ask anyone who wishes to, to toss a little shovel of soil in the hole (small toy shovels are inexpensive and work well for this). Place a commemorative plaque that students made out of clay or had donated, stating the type of tree, the date, and the occasion for which it was planted.
Materials Needed	ball and burlap tree suitable for local planting commemorative plaque small shovels topsoil
Vocabulary	**ball and burlap tree**—A ball and burlap tree is a tree that has been grown past a seedling size. It is planted with its roots and the surrounding ball of soil wrapped in burlap and reinforced with a rope or a wire basket.

Activity 30

LAUNCHING A POSTER CAMPAIGN

Subjects and Skills	Science, language arts, visual arts
Rationale	Even small gestures can garner results—putting up posters around the school may seem like a little thing, but it may bring ecological awareness to one person who was not thinking about it before and who may change his or her habits.
Objectives	Students will create posters displaying environmental messages and post them throughout the school.
Activity Preparation	1. Make sure it is OK to put student-made posters up throughout the school.
Activity Procedures	1. Have students work together in pairs or small groups to generate lists of ecological messages that could be put on posters to increase schoolwide awareness of the threats facing our environment.
	2. Come together as a class to share, critique, and combine statements.
	3. Have students each choose one statement or message to feature on a poster of their own design.
	4. Ask students to use the planning sheet to figure out exactly what their poster will look like before they begin working on the poster board.
	5. Allow students to use markers, paints, chalks, pastels, or any other supplies available to create their posters. Consider laminating the finished posters to preserve them and increase their beauty. (Laminating colorful displays sometimes makes the colors even more vivid.)
Materials Needed	poster board Launching a Poster Campaign Planning Sheet (one per student) various art supplies materials for hanging finished posters throughout the school
Vocabulary	**awareness**—to be knowledgeable, cognizant, and watchful

Name: _____ Date _____

Launching a Poster Campaign Planning Sheet

1. What will your poster say? _____

_____

_____

_____

_____

_____

_____

2. How can you illustrate this message? _____

_____

_____

_____

_____

_____

_____

3. What supplies will you need? _____

_____

_____

_____

_____

_____

4. Draw a pencil sketch of your poster design in the box below. Refer back to it as you create your finished work.

© Prufrock Press • *Hands-On Ecology*
This page may be photocopied or reproduced with permission for student use.

Activity 31

LITTER PICK-UP DAY

Subjects and Skills	Social studies
Rationale	Cleaning up litter around the schoolyard provides a clear visual of the impact kids can make when they put forth effort.
Objectives	Students will clean up the litter that is in and around their schoolyard.
Activity Preparation	1. This may be a good activity to use to spread the message of action. Contact local news media and tell them of your plans. Invite other classes to join you. Partner this activity with a tree-planting event or an Earth Day assembly. 2. Solicit parent or community volunteers to walk around with small groups of students as they clean.
Activity Procedures	1. Divide students into small groups assigned to an adult and give them an area to focus on. 2. Remind them that no piece of litter is too small to clean up; each piece contributes to the pollution of the grounds. 3. Give them plastic or rubber gloves, or have them bring in gardening gloves from home, and a plastic garbage bag. 4. Set a time limit and a location for groups to meet back, and let them go clean up. 5. Walk around, checking on groups and snapping pictures—what a great chronicle of student action!
Materials Needed	plastic, rubber, or gardening gloves (one pair per participant) garbage bags camera film
Vocabulary	**litter**—improperly disposed of waste **pollution**—environmental contamination

Activity 32

CONSERVATION PENNY DRIVE

Subjects and Skills	Science, language arts, mathematics, social studies
Rationale	Little acts can make big impacts and collecting something as small as a penny can generate big returns. Students can see firsthand how quickly pennies can add up.
Objectives	Students will organize a schoolwide, week-long penny drive to earn money to buy a portion of the rainforest, sponsor an endangered animal, or donate to an environmental agency of their choice.

Activity Preparation

1. Check with the administrators at your school to find out district fundraising policies and how money that is collected should be handled.
2. Contact the PTA to see if it would sponsor a popcorn party or some other small reward for the class that collects the most pennies.
3. Solicit volunteer counters and penny rollers from your students' parents or the PTA.

Activity Procedures

1. Promote the penny drive several weeks in advance to encourage people to save their pennies by sending home flyers telling about the project, sharing some environmental concerns, and telling parents what the money will be used for. Send these home weekly for about a month before the drive and daily the week before.
2. Make announcements at school letting kids know about the penny drive. You could turn it into a class competition where the class that brings in the most pennies by the end of the week will be rewarded with a popcorn party. Your students could (with the help of parent volunteers) count the pennies each day as they are brought in, keeping a running bar graph somewhere in the school where all students could see which class is in the lead.
3. Remind the kids using the morning announcements, or whatever means of communication your school uses, that pennies will be collected all week.
4. At the end of the week, count and roll whatever pennies haven't been rolled, and total them. Take them to a bank to exchange for cash and decide as a class what cause you would like to use your collection for.
5. As a class, decide what charity, organization, or cause to which you would like to donate the money you've collected.

Materials Needed   flyers
                    penny collection jars or buckets
                    penny rolls
                    poster board for making a school bar graph

Vocabulary   **nonprofit organization**—an organization whose purpose is something other than
              the generation of profit; usually to raise awareness of an issue and to help solve
              problems
              cause—a series of actions that help to advance the knowledge about or solution
              of a principle

Making a Contribution to Conservation

Activity 33

RECYCLING PROJECT

Subjects and Skills	Science, social studies
Rationale	Schools produce an enormous amount of recyclable waste including beverage containers, paper, and food containers. There is potential for schoolwide education of the benefits of conservation, community outreach, and fundraising, all using the recyclable waste that is already being generated.
Objectives	Students will create and implement a recycling program within their school.
Activity Preparation	1. This activity can be completed in conjunction with, in addition to, or in place of the tree planting activity in celebration of Earth Day. 2. Find out about and share area recycling programs and requirements.
Activity Procedures	1. Talk about what kind of project you want to involve yourselves in. 2. Your class could create an ongoing recycling project, or a one-time recycling drive, only collect certain types of recyclables, collect a variety of types, or develop this activity into whatever they wish. The ideas are limited only by the students' imaginations or your limits. 3. Use the planning sheet as a tool for this activity. 4. Create flyers and signs to advertise your project and its benefits.
Materials Needed	Recycling Program Planning Sheet poster board markers information about local recycling programs special recycling bins, if applicable trash cans for specific recyclables, if applicable
Vocabulary	**recycling**—to adapt or make ready for a new use

Recycling Program Planning Sheet

First, you need to decide what type of recycling program you want to start. Two ideas for types of recycling programs are described below.

Recycling Drive

This is a one-time program that eliminates the need for long-term storage of recyclables and may be easier to manage if time is limited. For this type of activity, you need to decide what you will be collecting and where the collection will take place. You'll need volunteers to help you sort and bundle the items and then adults to drive them to the recycling center. The key to this type of program is publicity. Contact local newspapers and radio stations, put up signs, and send flyers home with all of the students in your school. You'll need lots of people to know about this in advance so they can collect items and make arrangements to bring them up to your school.

In-School Recycling Program

This activity requires an ongoing crew of volunteers. You need to decide which types of recyclables you want to collect. Set up special collection bins or trash cans in various school locations, and educate the students in the school about their purpose. You may want to hold an assembly with the help of your school's administration to kickoff the program. You'll need volunteers (students or adults) to go through and bag the contents of the bins weekly, monthly, daily—however often they fill up—and adult volunteers to transport the collections to the recycling center. This option is a good way to get the whole school involved, encouraging daily recycling, which can hopefully transfer to students' homes.

What type of recycling program would you like to create?

_____

Name: _____ Date _____

Once you decide what type of program you're going to begin, you need to start planning the specifics of your program. Start by answering these questions:

1. What materials will you need in order to implement your program?

    _____

    _____

    _____

    _____

2. How will you recruit volunteers?

    _____

    _____

    _____

    _____

3. How will you generate publicity? If interviews will be given, will a student give them? The teacher? A student and teacher?

    _____

    _____

    _____

    _____

4. Which district administrators or staff do you need to clear your ideas with before implementing your program?

    _____

    _____

© Prufrock Press • *Hands-On Ecology*
This page may be photocopied or reproduced with permission for student use.

5. Does your principal approve? _____

6. Are there any district forms that need to be filled out before adding new bins or holding a community project?

   _____

   _____

   _____

   _____

7. What other problems or questions can you think of that would need to be solved or answered before you are able to implement your recycling program?

   _____

   _____

   _____

   _____

Activity 34

COMPOSTING

Subjects and Skills	Science, social studies
Rationale	Worms are "nature's recyclers," and as such can help solve some environmental waste problems.
Objectives	Students will learn how worms recycle waste and then produce nutrient-rich compost. Students will discuss how worms can help solve environmental problems.
Activity Preparation	1. Remember those worms from Activity 10? Now is the time to make them earn their keep! Before completing this activity, save several days worth of food scraps from your dinner table. Carrots, apple pieces or cores, coffee grounds, and eggshells all work well.
Activity Procedures	1. Pass out the Composting: What's the Point? handout and talk about the benefits of this Earth-saving idea.

Activity Procedures

1. Pass out the Composting: What's the Point? handout and talk about the benefits of this Earth-saving idea.
2. Prep the plastic container by punching air holes in the sides and lid.
3. Have students place 2–3 inches of a soil and sand mixture in the bottom of the box.
4. Have students add the garbage—remember to avoid cooked foods, especially meats, which take a very long time to break down and will rot, attracting unwanted pests and smells.
5. Then, have students place an additional 2 inches of soil or moistened newspaper strips on top of their fruit and vegetable waste.
6. Have students introduce their worm friends to their new home and job site.
7. Place the lid on the container and put the worm bin in a dark place (because the worms shy away from light) or cover the outside with dark paper.
8. Leave the container alone, for the most part, over the next few weeks. Check it periodically to make sure the soil stays damp. (It is important to keep it damp, not wet. You don't want water to pool at the bottom of the container.)
9. After the worms have worked for 2 weeks, ask your students to make predictions about what the soil and garbage within the container looks like. Have them record their predictions in their journals.
10. Then, with a small garden trowel, dig up a soil sample, making sure to dig all the way to the bottom so you get a sample from where the garbage had been. Spread this sample on a table where all of the students can observe.

11. Have students record their observations of the sample in their journals below their predictions. Explain that the worms take in the garbage and soil, digesting it and leaving behind a more nutrient-rich soil.

12. Ask your students to respond in their journals to the question, "How can worms help cut down on trash?"

13. Replace the soil sample and allow the worms to continue their work, checking every week or so.

14. The resulting soil can be used in classroom potted plants or school gardens. If you don't want to continue your composting project after your ecology lessons are over, ask another teacher or a parent with a garden if they want to keep it going at home or release the worms into your school gardens. Otherwise, ongoing composting can be fun for the kids. You could keep the bin working throughout the school year, periodically harvesting the rich compost and replacing bedding and food scraps.

Materials Needed	Composting: What's the Point? handout
	large plastic storage bin (Sterilite, Rubbermaid, or other large bins from discount stores work well. Make sure they are clear.)
	drill, ice pick, or other sharp object for making holes in the plastic.
	earthworms from Activity 10
	dirt or unfertilized soil
	food scraps
	damp newspaper strips
	field journals

Vocabulary	**composting**—the decomposition of organic matter

Name: _____ Date _____

Composting: What's the Point?

Composting is becoming more and more popular—in schools and in homes for garden use. But, what is the point, really? Why should we bother to mess around with garbage, worms, and keeping air circulating around it all? Several reasons, actually, some of which are listed here:

❧ Composting provides a partial solution to the overuse of our planet's limited landfills. By using nature's most basic recyclers, we can take an active role in limiting the dumping of trash and polluting our ecosphere.

❧ Composting provides a way not only of reducing the amount of waste that needs to be disposed of, but also of converting it into a product that is useful for gardening, landscaping, or house plants.

❧ By composting, we develop an ecological stewardship and take the "reuse, reduce, and recycle" concept one active step further.

❧ We can learn to view garbage as something organic and useful, rather than something "yucky" to be thrown away.

❧ Compost is better for your plants than store-bought fertilizers.

❧ It's free—you don't have to spend anything to compost on a small scale. Use an old plastic container, get some dirt from the backyard, dig up some worms and put in some scraps of food. Mix it around and mist it daily and you'll have some fresh compost for your houseplants in no time.

❧ It's fun! Learning about worms, playing with them, measuring them, racing them—worms are very interesting to learn about and you have your own little worm farm handy anytime you want to check them out.

© Prufrock Press • *Hands-On Ecology*
This page may be photocopied or reproduced with permission for student use.

Building Your Compost Pile

1. Prep the plastic container by punching air holes in the sides and lid.
2. Place 2–3 inches of a soil and sand mixture in the bottom of the box.
3. Add your garbage—remember to avoid cooked foods, especially meats, which take a very long time to break down and will rot, attracting unwanted pests and smells.
4. Place an additional 2 inches of soil or moistened newspaper strips on top of your fruit and vegetable waste.
5. Introduce your worm friends to their new home and job site.
6. Place the lid on the container and put the worm bin in a dark place (because the worms shy away from light) or cover the outside with dark paper.
7. Leave the container alone, for the most part, over the next few weeks. Check it periodically to make sure the soil stays damp. (It is important to keep it damp, not wet. You don't want water to pool at the bottom of the container.)
8. Remove the nutrient-rich soil as needed. Allow the worms to continue their work, checking every week or so.
9. The resulting soil can be used in classroom potted plants or school gardens. You could keep the bin working throughout the school year, periodically harvesting the rich compost and replacing bedding and food scraps.

Chapter

7

Creating a Wildlife Garden

Now is the time to make a beautiful and permanent contribution to your schoolyard by turning the observation site you used during part of this unit into a garden area designed to attract a variety of wildlife for students to learn about and enjoy. The schoolyard obliterates a piece of land that was once the home to a multitude of flora and fauna specifically adapted to this area. Remember that each organism occupies a niche, and by continuing to build, humans are forcing animals to leave their habitats. This is one way we can help to provide a continued place for organisms within their already defined niches.

It is important to remember that you are not cultivating gardens that will win acclaim and awards; the primary goal is to nurture a love of the environment and its life in your students. Therefore, it is imperative that students have the biggest role in the designing of the layout of their wildlife garden. A schoolyard wildlife garden should provide animals with food, water, shelter, and a place to safely raise their young.

This section (Activities 35–38) includes projects to help provide each of these basic elements to your garden in an attractive, fun way for kids. Let them allow their creativity to run free. You'll be impressed with the way things turn out, and you will be providing your school with a place to bring students and enjoy nature, wildlife, and sound ecological practices. What a lovely tribute to our planet, and a real-life application of the premises taught throughout this unit.

Activity 35

MAKING A CONTRACT WITH NATURE

Subjects and Skills	Science, language arts
Rationale	Children need to understand that everyone can make a difference and have a positive impact on their environments.
Objectives	Students will make a contract to help make steps to impact their environment.
Activity Preparation	1. Brainstorm with the class all the ways students can contribute locally to their environment.
Activity Procedures	1. Together as a class, create a "Contract With Nature" on chart paper.
	2. Have students come up with statements to add to it. For example:
	❀ I promise to recycle.
	❀ I will not cut down trees unnecessarily.
	❀ I will respect the wildlife in my backyard.
	3. Have each child sign the large classroom contract and display it in the room.
	4. Encourage them to copy it on notebook paper and include a signed copy in their field journal.
Materials Needed	chart paper notebook paper field journals
Vocabulary	**contract**—an agreement between two or more parties

Activity 36
BUILDING A HABITAT PILE

Subjects and Skills	Science
Rationale	Taking an active role in the preservation of animal homes and habitats can foster a lifelong ecological awareness in students.
Objectives	The students will construct a habitat pile in their observation site using natural materials found outside.
Activity Preparation	1. Decide where you will create your wildlife garden. Perhaps you want to turn the observation site you've been using into a haven for wildlife and a place future students can come and enjoy nature—it could be your contribution to encouraging ecological awareness in your school community. 2. Collect logs, sticks, and brush to tote out to your site.
Activity Procedures	1. Designate one area in your class's garden site to house the habitat pile. This will attract animals like insects, lizards, garter snakes, and other small creatures. Birds that build their nests near the ground may even come to live there. They will have shelter and be near lots of tasty insects to keep them happy. 2. Have a student criss-cross your logs to form the base of your pile. 3. Ask other students to lean the sticks and brush in a decorative way against the logs. Weave them together to keep them secure and safe for the animals that will call it home. Raffia or yarn could be used to do this or just use the sticks and brush. 4. Ask the groundskeeper to keep the grass long around this habitat pile. You and your students could be responsible for trimming the grasses if they get too high. 5. Have your students illustrate the finished pile in their field journals once it is built. Revisit it several times a week over the next few months to see what kinds of creatures have taken up residency.
Materials Needed	sticks, twigs, logs, brush raffia or yarn field journals
Vocabulary	**habitat pile**—a heap of garden debris that becomes a haven for wildlife

Activity 37

THIS PLACE IS FOR THE BIRDS

Subjects and Skills	Science, mathematics
Rationale	Taking an active role in the preservation of animal homes and habitats can foster a lifelong ecological awareness in students.
Objectives	Students will construct and place nesting boxes and feeders in their wildlife garden.
Activity Preparation	1. Solicit parent help for building day, along with donations for supplies.
	2. Decide which of the projects you are able to complete and assemble all of the necessary supplies.
Activity Procedures	1. Divide the students into small groups, assigning each to a parent-helper. Distribute the project instruction sheets, a different one to each group, and have them build their birding equipment.
	2. Once the platforms, feeders, and nesting boxes are complete, fill them with food or water and scatter them around your wildlife garden site. *Note:* If there are no trees near or in your site, you will need poles to support your feeders and boxes.
	3. Ask students to sketch the piece of equipment they helped to create.
	4. Over the next few weeks, give students time to sit quietly, observe, and illustrate their designated piece of equipment.
Materials Needed	field journals
	additional materials will depend on the objects you choose to construct; see the individual project sheets for more information
Vocabulary	**bird feeder**—an outdoor device that supplies food for wild birds
	nesting box—an artificial nesting structure
	nectar—a sugary substance produced by plants
	suet—animal fats fed to birds

Milk Carton Birdfeeder

Materials Needed

✿ Half gallon cardboard milk carton, empty and clean
✿ Ruler
✿ Scissors
✿ Hole punch
✿ String or yarn
✿ Bird seed

Procedures

1. Using your ruler, mark a line 2 ½ inches up on two adjoining sides.
2. Using your ruler, mark a line 2 ½ inches down from the top on the same two adjoining sides.
3. Cut the sides off between the marked lines so your carton resembles the picture.
4. Using a small hole punch, make two holes on the top of the milk carton.
5. Put string through the holes and tie to a tree or pole in your observation site.
6. Fill the bottom of the carton with birdseed.

© Prufrock Press • *Hands-On Ecology*
This page may be photocopied or reproduced with permission for student use.

Name: _____ Date _____

Fruit and Vegetable Feeders

Materials Needed

- ✿ Ears of corn
- ✿ Apples
- ✿ Oranges
- ✿ Small pieces of fruit like apples, oranges, grapes, raisins, dried cranberries, tomatoes, peaches, and nectarines
- ✿ Wooden kabob skewers
- ✿ Peanut butter
- ✿ Birdseed
- ✿ String, yarn, or twine

Procedures

To prepare the corn:

1. Peel the husks downward, leaving them attached.
2. Remove the silk.
3. Use your string to tie the husks together below the corn and hang from a tree.

For apple or orange feeders:

1. Cut apples or oranges in half.
2. Spread peanut butter on the peel side.
3. Roll in birdseed.
4. Using a wooden skewer, thread a piece of string or twine on your apple and hang it from a tree in your observation site.

To make Bird Kabobs

1. Thread pieces of dried and fresh fruit on wooden skewers.
2. In the middle of your kabob, tie a piece of string or twine and hang your kabob from a tree.

String a Garden Garland

1. Cut peaches, nectarines, or apples in thin slices.
2. String the fruit slices and dried cranberries or raisins on string, yarn, or twine.
3. Drape on tree branches, in shrubs, and all around your wildlife garden.

© Prufrock Press • Hands-On Ecology
This page may be photocopied or reproduced with permission for student use.

Pinecone Bird Feeder

Materials Needed

- ✿ Large, open pinecone
- ✿ Suet or peanut butter
- ✿ Rolled oats or cornmeal
- ✿ Birdseed
- ✿ Small pieces of dried fruit
- ✿ Twine, string, or yarn

Procedures

1. Mix ½ cup suet or peanut butter with 2 ½ cups cornmeal or rolled oats.
2. Stir in ½ cup dried fruit, and mix until blended well.
3. Tie your twine, string, or yarn to your pinecone.
4. Cover the pinecone with the food mixture.
5. Roll it in birdseed.
6. Tap off any excess seed and hang your feeder from a tree outside.

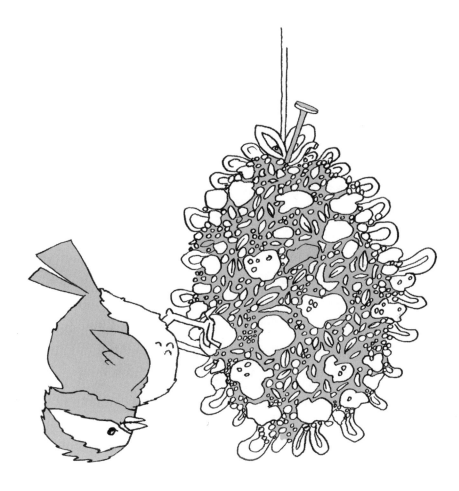

© Prufrock Press • *Hands-On Ecology*
This page may be photocopied or reproduced with permission for student use.

Name: _____ Date _____

Log Suet Feeder

Materials Needed

- ✿ Thick branch or piece of a log (between 4–8 inches thick)
- ✿ Drill with a 1 or 1 ½ inch diameter bit
- ✿ Large eye bolt
- ✿ Sturdy piece of rope

Procedures

1. Drill several 1-inch deep holes in various places around the log. (This is a job for parents or the teacher.)
2. Screw a large eyebolt in the top of the log.
3. Plug each hole with a suet mixture (Either store bought or the same mixture used on the pinecone bird feeders.)
4. Hang your log feeder from a strong tree or pole.

© Prufrock Press • *Hands-On Ecology*
This page may be photocopied or reproduced with permission for student use.

Name: _____ Date _____

Hummingbird Feeder

Materials Needed

- ❀ Clean, dry baby food jar
- ❀ Colorful paper or plastic pieces
- ❀ Hot glue gun
- ❀ Hammer
- ❀ Nail
- ❀ Hummingbird nectar

Procedures

1. Remove lid from the jar.
2. Have an adult hot glue colorful plastic or paper petals around the lid to make your feeder appealing to these color-loving birds.
3. Using the hammer and nail, make 4 or 5 small holes along one edge of the lid, making sure no sharp edges are exposed.
4. Pour your nectar into the jar and place the lid tightly on top.
5. Tie a long string or colorful piece of yarn around the neck of the jar and hang from a tree.

Bird Food Recipes

Hummingbird Nectar
- ✿ Combine 4 cups boiling water with 1 cup sugar.
- ✿ Let cool in the refrigerator.
- ✿ Fill hummingbird feeders or place in tiny, clean bottles like used vanilla bottles or saltshakers. Leave the lids off and tie them to trees with colorful yarn or pipe cleaners.

Peanut Butter Suet
- ✿ Gather the following materials:
  - ❏ 1 cup peanut butter
  - ❏ 1 cup lard
  - ❏ 2 cups quick cook oats
  - ❏ 2 cups cornmeal
  - ❏ 1–2 cups flour
  - ❏ small containers like empty margarine or yogurt containers
- ✿ Over a stove or hot plate, melt the lard and peanut butter in a pan.
- ✿ Stir in other ingredients, adding flour until it is no longer runny.
- ✿ Fill small, plastic containers and cool in the freezer (or cool in the refrigerator and "mush" the cooled suet into your log feeder).

Stuffed Bird Loaf
- ✿ Set a large loaf of dense, whole-grain bread out overnight.
- ✿ The next day, cut off one heel and hollow out the soft inside of the loaf.
- ✿ Crumble this up and scatter it around your wildlife garden.
- ✿ Stuff the inside of the loaf with a mixture of peanut butter, cornmeal, nuts, and dried fruit until it is almost overflowing.
- ✿ Set it out on a stump or platform feeder in your wildlife garden.

Milk Carton Nesting Box

Materials Needed
- ✿ Empty, clean milk carton
- ✿ Masking tape
- ✿ Brown paint or shoe polish
- ✿ Wire for hanging

Procedures
1. Cover the entire milk carton with masking tape—overlap it so none of the carton shows.
2. Rub on paint or shoe polish to color the carton like bark. Let it dry completely.
3. Decide what type of bird you want to attract. The following chart shows some specifications for attracting different types of birds.

Species	Height of entrance above floor	Diameter of entrance hole	Height of nest box from the ground
Bluebird	6 inches	1 ½ inches	5–10 feet
Chickadee	6–8 inches	1 ⅛ inches	6–15 feet
Titmouse	6–8 inches	1 ¼ inches	6–15 feet
Robin	8 inches	1 side open	6–15 feet
Barn Swallow	6 inches	1 side open	8–10 feet

4. Cut your entrance hole.
5. Make several small holes in the bottom of the carton to allow rainwater to drain.
6. Make several small holes in the top of the carton to allow condensation to escape, as well.
7. Thread the wire through the top of the carton and hang the nest box from a tree.

© Prufrock Press • *Hands-On Ecology*
This page may be photocopied or reproduced with permission for student use.

Name: _____ Date _____

Terra Cotta Pot Birdbath

Materials Needed

- ✿ 12-inch pot
- ✿ 14-inch pot
- ✿ 16-inch pot
- ✿ 18–20-inch diameter terra cotta saucer
- ✿ Silicone adhesive or caulk gun
- ✿ Acrylic paint
- ✿ Mosaic tiles, shells, or other decorative items
- ✿ Polyurethane or acrylic sealer

Procedures

1. Invert the pots on top of each other, securing them to one another with your adhesive.
2. Attach the saucer to the top with your adhesive.
3. Your birdbath can be used this way, it can be decorated using the adhesive to attach mosaic tiles or shells, or it can be painted and sealed with polyurethane.
4. Put your birdbath in your wildlife garden and fill the saucer with water.

© Prufrock Press • *Hands-On Ecology*
This page may be photocopied or reproduced with permission for student use.

Activity 38

BEE BOXES AND SPIDER SPACES

Subjects and Skills	Science, mathematics
Rationale	Taking an active role in the preservation of animal homes and habitats can foster a lifelong ecological awareness in students.
Objectives	Students will construct and place homes for a variety of animals in their wildlife garden.
Activity Preparation	1. Again, solicit parent help for building day and donations for supplies. 2. Decide which of the projects you are able to complete and assemble all of the necessary supplies.
Activity Procedures	1. Divide the students into small groups, assigning each to a parent-helper. Distribute the project instruction sheets, a different one to each group, and have them build their animal homes. 2. Distribute your homes throughout your wildlife garden, nestling toad houses in high grass, placing butterfly boxes high on poles or trees, spreading spider homes about, and so forth. 3. Ask students to sketch the piece of equipment they helped to create. 4. Over the next few weeks, give students time to sit quietly, observe, and illustrate their designated piece of equipment.
Materials Needed	field journals additional materials will depend on the objects you choose to construct; see the individual project sheets for more information
Vocabulary	**community**—a group of organisms sharing space **population**—the number of inhabitants in specific regions

Name: _____ Date _____

Bee Boxes

These small houses will provide cover for bees and a place for them to raise their young. These houses usually attract the Orchard Mason Bee, which does not nest, but lives in established holes it finds in wood. The male cannot sting and the female rarely stings. You can find out more about these interesting insects by visiting the following Web sites:

http://gardening.wsu.edu/library/inse006/inse006.htm

http://www.marchbiological.com/L/mason_bee.html

Materials Needed

- ✿ Drill with bits of various sizes
- ✿ Scrap lumber or wooden blocks
- ✿ Chicken wire
- ✿ Staple gun

Procedures

1. Ask a parent or teacher to take your piece of lumber and drill holes 3 or 4 inches deep, but not all the way through the wood.
2. Cover the holes with chicken wire. Have an adult secure it with the staple gun.
3. Secure the bee houses to trees, fence posts, or poles. **Do not disturb the bee houses once they are in place.**

Name: _____ Date _____

Ladybug Lair

This little round beetle, one of the world's most recognized insect, comes in red, orange, yellow, brown, tan, or gray. Most often seen with spots on its back, it can also have stripes. These are nice additions to any garden as they eat mites and aphids—insects that can be harmful to flowers. You can learn more about ladybugs at these Web sites:

http://www.nysaes.cornell.edu/ent/biocontrol/predators/ladybintro.html
http://ohioline.osu.edu/hyg-fact/2000/2002.html
http://www.marchbiological.com/L/ladybug.html

Materials Needed
✿ Oatmeal container or another round container with a lid
✿ Acrylic paint
✿ Polyurethane or spray sealer
✿ Craft knife
✿ Wire

Procedures
1. Decorate the container with your acrylic paints and let dry.
2. Seal the container with polyurethane or an acrylic sealer.
3. Have a parent or teacher help you cut a small, thin window at the top of the container and a door at the bottom.
4. Hang your house from a tree using your wire.

© Prufrock Press • *Hands-On Ecology*
This page may be photocopied or reproduced with permission for student use.

Toad Town

Set up a town for this helpful garden guest! Toads eat a variety of garden pests like slugs, mosquitoes, and other insects, and can keep the unwanted bugs under control. All toads have short, stubby, chunky bodies, although the coloring may be different depending on the species. To find out more about toads, check out these Web sites:

http://www.fcps.k12.va.us/StratfordLandingES/Ecology/mpages/american_toad.htm

http://museum.gov.ns.ca/mnh/nature/frogs/toad.htm

Materials Needed
- ✿ Various sized clay pots
- ✿ Various sized clay saucers
- ✿ Different sized stones
- ✿ Acrylic paints
- ✿ Acrylic sealer
- ✿ Mosaic tiles, shells, or other decorative items
- ✿ Hot glue gun

Procedures
1. Use your paint to decorate the pots. (You could have some fun and paint them to resemble different buildings in your community.) You could also ask a parent or teacher to hot glue tiles, shells, or other decorative items onto the pot.
2. Out in your wildlife garden, place your "buildings" upside-down, with the edge resting on a rock, leaving enough room for a toad to sneak inside to get out of the day's heat. You could also chip off a chunk of the pot at the rim, making a doorway.
3. Put the saucer near the buildings, partially buried and filled with water. This will be a nice, cool dipping pond (or neighborhood pool) for your toads.
4. Finally, if you are feeling very creative, you can make a mini fence to enclose your "toad town." You could also make little signs identifying your buildings, pond, or pool.

This page may be photocopied or reproduced with permission for student use.

Lizard Lounge

Like all cold-blooded animals, lizards rely on outside sources to heat their bodies. Because of this, lizards need basking areas to relax and soak up the sun's heat. Rock piles and walls are wonderful areas to observe these interesting little animals as they rest. They can quickly find shelter from predators by scurrying under the rock they are basking on. Find out more about these funny creatures by navigating the following sites to see what lizards can be found in your area:

http://eduscapes.com/nature/lizard/index1.htm

http://www.herper.com/reptiles/lizards.html

http://www.audubon.org/local/sanctuary/corkscrew/Wildlife/Lizards.html

Materials Needed

✿ Large 20–24 inch diameter terra cotta pot
✿ Irregularly shaped rocks of various sizes
✿ Cinder blocks
✿ Bricks

Procedures

1. Fill your clay pot with different-shaped rocks, leaving many cracks and crevices, and set it in your wildlife garden near bushes, walls, or spots that are lit at night.

2. Scatter cinder blocks and bricks, along with additional rocks, in a jumbled pile, leaving many hiding places for lizards to hide from predators.

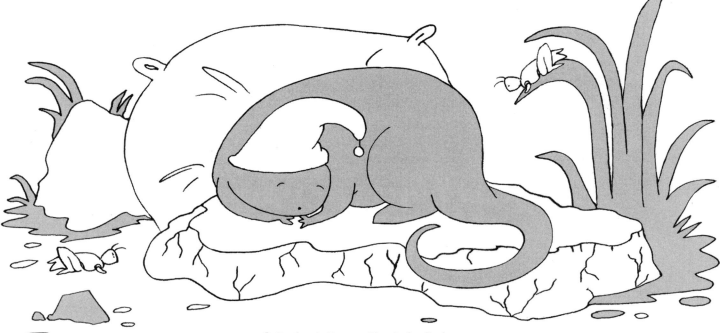

Spider Spaces

Another beneficial garden citizen is the spider. Spiders trap harmful insects in their webs and eat their tasty treats when they are hungry. Spiders come in many species, and spin different types of webs. You can find out about several different species at the following Web sites:

http://ohioline.osu.edu/hyg-fact/2000/2060.html

http://insects.tamu.edu/extension/bulletins/l-1787.html

http://insected.arizona.edu/spiderinfo.htm

Materials Needed

❁ Old window panes, picture frames, bike tires, other open recyclables

❁ Popsicle sticks

❁ Wood glue or hot glue gun

Procedures

1. Your recyclables should be placed in sheltered areas in your wildlife garden, leaning against trees, walls, or shrubs.

2. To make a spider space out of popsicle sticks, plan your design on paper first by drawing the shape you want it to be. Make sure to leave a large open space in the middle and have sticks on one side forming a "pole" so you can secure it in the ground.

3. Lay out your sticks in the arrangement you will be gluing them.

4. Glue them together.

5. When they are completely dry, put them in a relatively sheltered space in your wildlife garden.

© Prufrock Press • *Hands-On Ecology*
This page may be photocopied or reproduced with permission for student use.

Appendix: Resources

Books

Below is a list of books to use as read-alouds, additional resources, and just to build a classroom library. Use this as a starting point—some suggestions to get you going—but dig deeper. There are hundreds of wonderful books out there about various ecosystems, habitats, animals, plants, and issues our environment faces.

Asch, F. (1994). *The Earth and I.* New York: Gulliver Green.

Atkins, J. (1995). *Aani and the tree huggers.* New York: Lee & Low Books.

Atkins, J. (2000). *Girls who looked under rocks.* Nevada City, CA: DAWN Publications.

Baker, J. (2004). *Home.* New York: Greenwillow.

Beadlee, D. M. (2004). *The day the trash came out to play.* South Pasadena, CA: Ezra's Earth.

Burnie, D. (2001). *Earth watch: Protecting our planet.* New York: DK Publishing.

Caduto, M. J. (1997). *Earth tales from around the world.* Golden, CO: Fulcrum.

Carlson, L. (1992). *EcoArt!* Charlotte, VT: Williamson Company.

Collard, S. (2000). *Action for nature.* Berkeley, CA: Heyday Books.

Cornell, J., & Muir, J. (2000). *John Muir: My life with nature.* Nevada City, CA: DAWN Publications.

Cronin, D. (2003). *Diary of a worm.* New York: Joanna Colter Books.

Dobson, D. (1997). *Can we save them?: Endangered species of North America.* Watertown, MA: Charlesbridge.

Elliot, M. (2001). *Fun with recycling.* London: Southwater.

Fleischman, P. (2002). *Weslandia*. Cambridge, MA: Candlewick Press.

Goldsworthy, A. (1990). *A collaboration with nature*. New York: Harry N. Abrams.

Jenkins, S. (1997). *What do you do when something wants to eat you?* Boston: Houghton Mifflin.

Jenkins, S. (2006). *Almost gone: The world's rarest animals*. New York: HarperCollins.

Koontz, R. M. (1998). *The complete backyard nature activity book*. New York: McGraw-Hill.

Lauber, P. (1994). *Be a friend to trees*. New York: HarperTrophy.

Lavies, B. (1993). *Compost critters*. New York: Dutton Juvenile.

London, J. (2005). *Giving thanks*. Cambridge, MA: Candlewick Press.

Lorbiecki, M. (2005). *Planet patrol*. Minnetonka, MN: Two-Can.

Lowery, L. (2003). *Earth Day*. Minneapolis, MN: Carolrhoda Books.

Markle, S., & Markle, W. (1998). *Gone forever: An alphabet of extinct animals*. New York: Atheneum.

Mills, A., & Attenborough, D. (2005). *Animals like us*. New York: DK Publishing.

Morgan, S., & Harlow, R. (2002). *Energy and power*. New York: Kingfisher.

Needham, B. (1999). *Ecology crafts for kids*. New York: Sterling.

Peet, B. (1966). *Farewell to shady glade*. New York: Houghton Mifflin.

Pfiffner, G. (1995). *Earth-friendly holidays*. Hoboken, NJ: John Wiley and Sons.

Pringle, L. (2003). *Global warming*. San Francisco: Chronicle Books.

Pringle, L. (2000). *The environmental movement*. New York: HarperCollins.

Rogers, S. (1998). *Earthsong*. New York: Dutton Children Books.

Schimmel, S. (1994). *Dear children of the Earth*. Minnetonka, MN: Northword Press.

Schnetzler, P. (2004). *Earth Day birthday*. Nevada City, CA: DAWN Publications.

Schwartz, L. (1990). *The Earth book for kids*. Santa Barbara, CA: Learning Works.

Seuss, D. (1971). *The lorax*. New York: Random House.

Stetson, E. (2004). *Kids' easy-to-create wildlife habitats*. Nashville, TN: Williamson Books.

Sussman, A. (2000). *Dr. Art's guide to planet Earth*. White River Junction, VT: Chelsea Green.

Suzuki, D., & Vanderlinden, K. (2001). *Eco-fun*. Vancouver, BC, Canada: Douglas & McIntyre.

Tolan, S. (1990). *John Muir*. New York: Morehouse.

Van Allsburg, C. (1990). *Just a dream*. New York: Houghton Mifflin.

Magazines

Below is a list of magazine titles and their Web sites to get you started as you build your resource library. They will provide nice background information and wonderful pictures for your students to enjoy. The Web sites should provide you with all of the information you need to subscribe to these magazines.

Audubon Magazine
http://magazine.audubon.org

ChicaDEE
http://www.owlkids.com/chickaDEE

Chirp
http://www.owlkids.com/chirp

Cousteau Kids
http://www.cousteaukids.org

Current Science
http://www.weeklyreader.com/teens/current_science

Earth Island Journal
http://www.earthisland.org

E/The Environmental Magazine
http://www.emagazine.com

Green Teacher Magazine
http://www.greenteacher.com

National Geographic Kids
http://www.nationalgeographic.com/kids

National Parks Conservation Association Magazine
http://www.npca.org/magazine

National Wildlife Magazine
http://www.nwf.org/nationalwildlife

Odyssey: Adventures in Science
http://www.odysseymagazine.com

Owl
http://www.owlkids.com/owl

Ranger Rick
http://www.nwf.org/gowild

Science and Children
http://www.nsta.org/elementaryschool#journal

Science Scope
http://www.nsta.org/middleschool#journal

Science Weekly
http://www.scienceweekly.com

Sierra Magazine
http://www.sierraclub.org/sierra

Talking Leaves
http://www.talkingleaves.org

Yes Mag: Canada's Science Magazine for Kids
http://www.yesmag.bc.ca

Web sites

Below is a short list to get you going on the Web. The best thing to do, though, is to plug the topic you are most interested in gaining more information about and keywords related to that information into a search engine like Google. Be careful, however: There are so many excellent Web sites devoted to environmentalism that it is easy to lose sight of the purpose for your research as you enjoy the stories, anecdotes, and photography.

Ecology WWW

http://pbil.univ-lyon1.fr/Ecology/Ecology-WWW.html
This is a great resource for teachers as it contains an extensive list of additional Web links.

Envirolink Library

http://www.envirolink.org/EnviroLink_Library
Everything you need to know about the field of ecology. Also includes resources and graphics for students.

Journey North
http://www.learner.org/jnorth
An interactive site that tracks the migratory habits of select animals.

The Butterfly Website
http://butterflywebsite.com
Learn all about butterflies here.

U.S. Environmental Protection Agency
http://www.epa.gov
This is the homepage for the U.S. Environmental Protection Agency.

Amazing Environmental Organization Web Directory
http://www.webdirectory.com
This is a wonderful search engine for everything environmental.

Monarch Watch
http://MonarchWatch.org
Keep an eye on the monarchs of the world.

Caribbean Conservation Corporation & Sea Turtle Survival League
http://www.cccturtle.org
Learn about these fascinating ocean animals.

EPA's Environmental Kids Club
http://www.epa.gov/kids
The EPA's "just for kids" place.

World Biomes
http://www.ucmp.berkeley.edu/glossary/gloss5/biome
This Web site is an introduction to the major biomes on Earth.

About the Author

A gifted intervention specialist for students in grades 2 and 3, Colleen Kessler feels strongly that all students should be challenged to experience and learn new things every day. Colleen received her bachelor's degree in elementary education from Cleveland State University and her master's degree in gifted education from Kent State University. Colleen has written several educational resource books for teachers of advanced learners, as well as test questions and passages for publishers like CTBS/McGraw-Hill. She lives in Ohio, where she continues to write for publication in the educational field while teaching, working with, and advocating for gifted children.